Inclusive Learning and Educational Equity

Volume 1

This book series reflects on the challenges of inclusive education as a strategy for improving educational equity, and includes in-depth analyses of disparities in education and the mechanisms by which they operate. It studies the development of educational processes and pedagogical interventions that respond to the tensions between education policies that promote competition and those designed to promote inclusion at individual, classroom, school, district, national, and international levels. Finally, it presents research and development activities in teacher education that respond to the challenges of preparing teachers for the changing demographic of schooling. Increasingly throughout the world, a broad concept of inclusive education has begun to emerge as a strategy for achieving basic education for all learners regardless of cultural, developmental or linguistic differences. Although considered an important aspect of a global human rights agenda supported by the multilateral Global Partnership for Education, basic education is a complex endeavour that is subject to the forces of globalization, and the exclusionary pressures associated with migration, mobility, language, ethnicity, disability, and intergenerational poverty. The reciprocal links between these factors and educational underachievement has led to an increasing interest in the development of inclusive education as a strategy for improving educational equity. By addressing these and related issues, this series contributes important advances in knowledge about the enactment of inclusive education. This series: Offers a critical perspective on current practice Stimulates and challenges further developments for the field Explores global disparities in educational provision and compares developments Provides a welcome addition to the literature on inclusive education.

More information about this series at http://www.springer.com/series/13450

Jennifer Spratt

Wellbeing, Equity and Education

A Critical Analysis of Policy Discourses of Wellbeing in Schools

Springer

Jennifer Spratt
School of Education
University of Aberdeen
Aberdeen, UK

Inclusive Learning and Educational Equity
ISBN 978-3-319-50064-5 ISBN 978-3-319-50066-9 (eBook)
DOI 10.1007/978-3-319-50066-9

Library of Congress Control Number: 2017930185

Printed on acid-free paper

This Springer imprint is published by Springer Nature
The registered company is Springer International Publishing AG
The registered company address is: Gewerbestrasse 11, 6330 Cham, Switzerland

Series Editor's Preface

The idea that every child has a good experience of schooling is central to the inclusion agenda because a good experience of schooling is associated with positive outcomes. But claiming that a school is inclusive because it enrols a diverse student population, or a high proportion of students with additional support needs, is insufficient to ensure that all students have a good experience of schooling or learning or that good outcomes will follow. Indeed, the underachievement of certain groups of students has led to a renewed focus on interventions that aim to 'close the gap' between the lowest and highest achievers as an issue of fairness and social justice in education. But concepts such as inclusion, achievement, fairness and social justice are abstract and contentious and some would argue incompatible and too closely aligned with a focus on academic outcomes only. In response, the idea of wellbeing has come to be seen as both an important condition and outcome of learning.

This book provides a welcome addition to the literature on inclusive education that does not shy away from the complexities of simultaneous and contrasting wellbeing discourses that range from producing economically useful citizens to considerations of the role of the school in enhancing one's capacity to lead what one considers to be a good life. Through an exploration of these potential outcomes and the role that schools and teachers play in influencing them, *Wellbeing, Equity and Education: A Critical Analysis of Policy Discourses of Wellbeing in Schools* offers a broad conceptual engagement with concepts of inclusion, achievement, fairness and social justice which help to address the challenges of inclusive education as a strategy for improving equity outcomes.

The ideals of inclusive education make promises that many schools struggle to fulfil. For many years, approaches to policy practice and research about inclusion and equity have been dominated by the needs of individuals and groups who might be excluded or marginalised from schooling. This book helps to reframe debates about inclusive education through a deepening understanding of the role that schools and those who work in them play in the wellbeing of children and young people. By focusing on the 'what' rather than the 'who' of inclusive education, the book offers a critical perspective on the 'wellbeing agenda' in education that not only inaugurates this new series on inclusive learning and educational equity but sets a course for advances in knowledge about the enactment of inclusive education.

University of Edinburgh, Edinburgh, UK Lani Florian

Acknowledgements

I would like to thank Professors Lani Florian and Martyn Rouse for their support throughout this project. Their knowledge and wisdom, patience and humour have contributed immeasurably to my work. I am also grateful to colleagues in the University of Aberdeen School of Education for their encouragement of this endeavour. I am indebted to each of the 25 interviewees for generously sharing their time and their thoughts with me. Without their participation, this project would not have been possible. Special thanks to Roderick Scott, for creating the fantastic set of linocuts of 'wellbeing' specially for this publication.

Information about the Artworks by Roderick Scott

Each chapter starts with a linocut print in which kite-flying images in different environments are used as a symbol of 'wellbeing'. The kite images have different designs and are at different stages of flight to represent diversity. The symbol of wellbeing is printed in different environments, urban, rural, on and around school buildings and outside classes and examination rooms. One print, in Chap. 7, does not contain kites. Entitled '6 Hours After Mindfulness', this represents situations where the personal is manipulated to serve the functional.

Contents

Chapter 1
Introduction

When addressing schools' responses to inequalities, discussions are often framed in terms of enhancing wellbeing (e.g. McLaughlin 2015). Indeed, the keynote speaker at a recent international conference claimed that schools are shifting from a focus on achievement to a focus on wellbeing (Hargreaves 2016). Drawing on a discourse

J. Spratt, *Wellbeing, Equity and Education*, Inclusive Learning and Educational Equity 1, DOI 10.1007/978-3-319-50066-9_1

analysis undertaken in Scotland, this book is aiming to show how the concept of wellbeing is utilised in educational contexts, and how this may, or may not, contribute to equity and social justice.

Wellbeing is undoubtedly an appealing term (Amerijckx and Humblet 2014) and is universally seen as a 'good thing' inviting and uniting support from many different constituencies (Ereaut and Whiting 2008). Yet, despite the intense interest in wellbeing, it remains an elusive concept which is open to a multiplicity of interpretations (Watson et al. 2012). The main task of this book is to disentangle the 'milling mass' (Jager and Maier 2009) of discourses which converge around the concept of wellbeing, to explore how they are invoked in relation to other purposes of schooling, and to identify the implications for social justice. By problematizing the 'taken for granted' discourse of wellbeing this analysis will reveal how, seemingly soft language can be used to mask harsher ideological purposes. At the same time, if differently viewed, the wellbeing agenda provides opportunities for education to enhance children's freedoms to identify and pursue what, for them, is a valuable life.

Wellbeing has emerged as a twenty-first century policy concern (although its philosophical origins are considerably older) and increasingly governments are seeing it as a matter for state concern. In the pursuit of better understanding and improvement, national measures of wellbeing have been reported annually in the UK since 2012 (Office for National Statistics 2016), childhood wellbeing has been the subject of international comparisons between rich countries (UNICEF Innocenti Research Centre 2007; UNICEF Office of Research 2013), and national indicators of children's wellbeing are reported annually in the USA (Federal Interagency Forum on Child and Family Statistics 2016). This has resulted in demands that schools take responsibility for the wellbeing of children, resulting in a proliferation of policies that extend the remit of schools into some very personal areas of children's lives. This represents a marked change from the late 1990s when research highlighted the lack of interest that UK schools showed in children's health (e.g. Mayall 1996).

Under the banner of wellbeing the state has noiselessly re-drawn the boundaries between home and school as children's feelings have become the legitimate responsibility of teachers. With little consultation, the government has extended its reach into the emotional lives of children. Moreover, schools are charged with compensating for difficulties caused by societal inequalities by addressing the wellbeing of children (Morrow and Mayall 2009). These changes have been ushered in with limited, although growing critique (e.g. Watson et al. 2012; Ecclestone and Hayes 2009b; Cigman 2012; Suissa 2008; Clack 2012; Humphrey 2013). This may be due to the unchallenged positive connotations associated with the word wellbeing, after all who could possibly be opposed to the wellbeing of children?

Of course, schools in have, for a long time, included health education in some format on their curriculum, teaching about sexual health, drug education, nutrition and so on. Similarly, physical education is a well-established staple of schooling. The new focus on wellbeing goes beyond learning *about* health, urging teachers to take a 'holistic' interest in the experience of the 'whole child'. This is a somewhat less tangible understanding of the teacher's responsibility which merges with the other activities of the school, as issues of emotions, relationships and rights, permeate the life and learning of the school.

New policy interventions are not introduced in a vacuum, they are received and responded to in the context of the existing processes, priorities, roles and values of education policy makers and practitioners (Spratt et al. 2013). In addition to examining how wellbeing is understood in policy and practice communities, this book explores how wellbeing policies in schools interact with the main business of schools i.e. teaching and learning. 'Learning' is viewed in its broadest sense to include the knowledge and skills of the formal curriculum alongside the less tangible development of dispositions, attitudes and character that schools seek to imbue in young people. In this sense the book will explore how the discourse of wellbeing can be linked to, interact with or be appropriated by the wider purposes of schooling.

Currently, most debates about wellbeing of children tend to highlight certain aspects of schooling. Variables such as educational outcomes in key subject areas, participation rates in education, school completion rates and college enrolment are used as objective indicators of childhood wellbeing in national and international surveys (UNICEF Office of Research 2013; Federal Interagency Forum on Child and Family Statistics 2016). Educational achievement and feelings of success are identified by young people themselves as important aspects of subjective wellbeing as are experiential aspects of schooling such as friendships, bullying, relations with teachers and stress from time pressure (The Children's Society 2015; Shucksmith et al. 2009). Yet missing from these analyses is any discussion of the educational activities of schooling. What is taught and how it is taught has received little attention in discussions of wellbeing, although recently in a large Australian study young people drew attention to pedagogical approaches that they felt impacted on their wellbeing (Simmons et al. 2015). This book seeks to analyse the complex relationships between discourses of wellbeing and learning, to reveal issues of power and control.

In focussing on *discourses* the book will deconstruct the 'taken for granted' concept of wellbeing and examine how it is understood and represented in the context of education policy. Drawing from Ereaut and Whiting (2008) it will demonstrate how the concept of wellbeing, as used in contemporary education policy, can be traced to several different academic and professional disciplines, emerging at various historical times. In some ways this makes it a useful concept for consensual interagency dialogue, as all professionals will claim to ascribe to childhood wellbeing. At the same time, it may give rise to confusion or conflict as different actors may not necessarily understand the term in the same way. In the educational context, I will argue, the discourses of other professional groups have migrated into education policy, and these interact with teaching and learning in complex ways (Spratt 2016).

In order to understand these discursive relationships, it is necessary to explore the multiple purposes of schooling. In a discussion of social justice in school we need to consider what it is we mean by equality. As Apple (2006) reminds us, education is a political act. There are fundamentally different ideologies jostling for position in education, each with their own perspectives on social justice and equality. An instrumental view of education sees its purpose in terms of employability, with equality addressed by enhancing access to the job market. Those who argue for a more intrinsic value of education in enriching the lives of children and young people in multiple ways would favour a view of social justice as inclusion in the community and access to opportunities to lead a life of value. Both of these ideologies can be identified as influencing contemporary educational thought, and they can also be distinguished in the way that they invoke discourses of wellbeing.

The Capability Approach, developed by Amartya Sen (2009) offers a theoretical perspective for thinking about wellbeing in the context of social justice which has informed a body of work in education (e.g. Walker 2006; Flores-Crespo 2007; Unterhalter and Walker 2007) and is an important tool for the analyses that take place in this book. Whilst the book examines multiple perspectives in this complex field, Sen's work is informative at several levels and is drawn on in detail throughout the work. Ultimately the Capability Approach provides a framework within which it is possible to draw some overarching conclusions in the final sections of the book.

Whilst the policy interest in children's wellbeing is international in scope, individual nations may respond differently, as they adopt the policies into their own national context, according to their unique histories, cultures, and contemporary priorities (Rizvi and Lingard 2010). Differences approaches can be seen between the four countries of the UK in how they invoke wellbeing in the educational context. The Welsh Government (2011) houses a web page entitled 'Well-being' identifying a clear link between wellbeing and learning, stating 'This section is home to our policies that promote a healthy and happy school. This aids the learning environment'. The Department of Education in Northern Ireland signalled its interest in childhood wellbeing by commissioning a review of childhood health and wellbeing by Queen's University, Belfast, resulting in the introduction of the 'Pupils Emotional Health and Wellbeing Programme', named 'iMatter' (Department of Education Northern Ireland 2014).

By contrast, the English government has moved away from its previous emphasis on children's wellbeing by dismantling of the 'Every Child Matters' policy in which emotional wellbeing was prominent (Department of Children, Schools and Families Department of Children and Schools 2003). However, despite the downgraded status of wellbeing in English policy, it is clear from a cursory tour of school websites that the discourse of wellbeing persists in terms of core values and school mission statements. Commonly, as schools present their public face they refer to such issues as school ethos, relationships, care, happiness, support and guidance. The idea that education is an emotional process has not been erased by the change in policy, instead as Ball, Maguire and Braun (2012) describe there is evidence of a discursive policy archive, whereby schools and teachers continue to draw from the discourses of previous policies even where they have been superseded.

In Scotland, there is a legal requirement on local authorities to ensure that all schools are health promoting (Scottish Government 2007a) and this is expressed in policy through the 'health and wellbeing' polices in the national 'Curriculum for Excellence' (Scottish Executive 2004). In addition to teaching *about* health and wellbeing, in the more traditional guise of health education, the 'Curriculum for Excellence' demands that health and wellbeing should be fostered 'across learning' (Scottish Government n.d.-a, n.d.-b). Health and wellbeing is described as 'the responsibility of all' and is expected to frame the whole learning process. The term 'learning *through* health and wellbeing' (my italics) is used in the guidelines accompanying the 'Curriculum for Excellence' to invoke this concept. The new relationship between two professional territories is encapsulated in the expression 'learning and health go hand in hand', (Scottish Health Promoting Schools Unit 2004).

So whilst the four countries of the UK illustrate different policy stances on the wellbeing of children, it is clear that this is nonetheless an issue of interest to educators across the UK, and beyond. Scotland makes a particularly interesting case for closer scrutiny because the health and wellbeing policies are so well developed, and clearly articulated in an array of curricular documents. The choice of Scotland as the focus for this work is not an attempt to criticise the Scottish Government for its approach to wellbeing in schools, indeed I would argue that the Scottish Government has been particularly innovative and creative in giving such a high priority to the wellbeing of its children. The detailed documentation has provided a golden opportunity to thoroughly research contemporary discourses of childhood wellbeing and the interconnections with other aspects of school life. The Scottish policy context invites an examination of issues which are of interest to educationalists more widely.

Like all other countries, Scotland looks to its schools to support its success in the international market economy, but at the same time it has a long and proud history of social democratic aspirations, particularly within education. This uneasy dualism, which is familiar to educators across the globe is writ large in Scottish politics, and in this situation the conflicting understandings of social justice are readily evident. Whilst readers may not be familiar with this national context, they may recognise how the Scottish situation can inform understandings of these issues in their own setting.

1.1 The Research Study

The study on which this book is based was a Critical Discourse Analysis (CDA) of the Scottish health and wellbeing policies, exploring the understandings and purposes of wellbeing in the school context as portrayed in written policy and in the spoken word of professionals. CDA is a methodological approach which explores issues of power within language, which is particularly appropriate when governments design interventions aimed at shaping children's emotions and behaviours. The nature of Critical Discourse Analysis is discussed in Chap. 2 and further methodological details are provided in an Appendix.

The study took place in two phases. Firstly, analysis of relevant policy texts in Scotland's 'Curriculum for Excellence' (Education Scotland n.d.) revealed the range of discursive actions of the health and wellbeing policy. This was followed by interviews with interviews with 25 professionals, both policy actors and teachers to examine how the policy discourses were recontextualised (Bernstein 2000) as they moved from the written documentation to the spoken language. The study provides evidence of how the new policy discourses were reshaped and reformed by the practitioners entrusted with implementation, as they brought their own experience and understandings to bear. Different representations were evident, often within the same institutions, that range from repeating policy, deepening the policy positions and reinterpreting policy from a different perspective. This shows how discourses shift and change, not always in the ways that the writers of policy may have anticipated.

The emphasis of the research was on those aspects of health and wellbeing that permeate school life, which are deemed by Scottish Government to be 'the responsibility of all'. These may be incorporated into the formal curriculum through cross curricular lessons (e.g. a geography lesson might include a consideration of the social wellbeing of a particular group of people) or they may be part of the general pedagogical approach or the ethos of the classroom. This study did not include topics that are directly taught through formal subjects such as food and nutrition, or physical education, so the analysis does not include, for example the home economics curriculum, or the biology syllabus.

1.2 The Structure of the Book

The start of this book will discuss some of the key concepts which underpin the arguments later in the book. The early chapters devote themselves to discussions of discourse and policy (Chap. 2), equity and schooling (Chap. 3) and the conceptualisation of wellbeing (Chap. 4). The tone of the book then becomes more critical as it demonstrates how wellbeing, learning and social justice interact, and how the discursive relationships between them can mobilised in support of different political agendas (Chap. 5). The book then moves to discuss in some detail the health and wellbeing policies of Scotland, with Chap. 6 examining the conceptualisation of wellbeing, Chap. 7 exploring the relationships between wellbeing and learning, and identifying the implications for social justice. Chapter 8 draws on interview data to show how discourses are recontextualised by teachers and policy actors, and demonstrates the way in which the discourses are reshaped and remodelled by different users of policy. Finally, in Chap. 9 the overall findings of the book are discussed and, drawing from the Capability Approach (Sen 2009) a model is suggested in which different perspectives can be drawn together to provide a way of integrating this jumble of perspectives into an understanding of the mutual relationships between wellbeing, teaching and learning that is congruent with a welfare-liberal understanding of justice.

The structure of the book is as follows:

Chapter 2 will act as an introduction key concepts relating to discourse and policy that will be used in later discussions. It is a generic introduction, for the reader who is unfamiliar with the study of these concepts.

Discourse will be discussed as the way that people represent their view of the world. The interests of this book in the social effects of discourse will be discussed, and the role of discourses in the influence of powerful groups will be examined. The relationships between ideology and discourse will be explored to demonstrate how dominant ideologies are propagated. The ways that discourses may act without the knowledge of the speaker, under the guise of 'common sense' language that has been naturalised in everyday speech will be discussed. The operation of multiple discourses simultaneously, which interact in complex ways (as in the case of wellbeing) will be explored. The concept of 'recontextualisation' will be introduced as discourses move from the policy making community to be adopted by the enactors of policy, to show how discourses are not static, but shift and change as they are interpreted and adopted in new contexts.

Education policy is discussed as a platform through which those in power can influence the discursive actions, and the behaviours of teachers and other professionals in schools, showing that there are powerful and competing influences on policy that can have far reaching effects on the experiences of children. This chapter provides a basis for the discussions of educational policies of wellbeing that follow.

Chapter 3 opens by raising a question of what meant by social justice in schools, by borrowing from Sen (1992) to ask 'Equality of What?' In exploring how we understand justice in education this chapter looks at what schooling is for.

It shows how the concept of liberalism has divergently evolved to give rise to seemingly oppositional ideological positions, of welfare-liberalism and neo-liberalism each of which demand different things from education. The former values the intrinsic value of education as a personal and democratic good, and would see social justice as fostering enrichment and fulfilment for all. The latter values education solely for its economic purposes and would frame social justice in terms of enhancing the skills, knowledge and personal attributes required for employment (human capital). This chapter discusses how both of these ideologies are at play in education, simultaneously, and explores the composite purposes of education, coupled with the implications for equity.

Amartya Sen's Capability Approach is introduced, framing social justice as the freedom to lead a life you have reason to value. In this view, the value of education in supporting individuals to become economically active is not forgotten, but this is seen to be a means to an end. Ultimately in this view, education serves to enhance opportunities to recognise and pursue those things that are value to the individual. This has considerable implications for education – and raises questions about what education for Capability would look like.

Chapter 4 will show how the term wellbeing, as used in the context of schooling, emerges from a range of professional and academic disciplines each with their own understanding of the meaning. Whilst this multi-disciplinary buy-in allows wellbeing to be the focus of inter-professional effort and discussion it can also lead to misunderstandings and confusion. Drawing from the work of Ereaut and Whiting (2008) five main discursive themes of wellbeing are identified and discussed. The discourse of physical health promotion focuses on health, and health related behaviours, such as diet exercise, and risky behaviours, and is often discussed within the context of choice. The psychological discourse of social and emotional literacy focuses on understanding and control of emotions and management of self in social situations. The discourse of care links education with the field of social care of children and is evident in interagency contexts. This theme is associated with the provision made for children by professionals. In the school context issues such as ethos, relationships and rights, are invoked, in the context of the 'whole child'. The philosophical discourse of flourishing derives from Aristotle's concept of eudaimonic happiness, which underpins the Capability Approach (Sen 2009). This is conceptualised by as leading a life one has reason to value. The emergent discourse of sustainability links environmental sustainability with human wellbeing, mediated by a discourse of social justice. Whist discussions of sustainability are not novel, school based discourses linking environmental and outdoor education to individual wellbeing is a newly emerging discourse. Whilst it can be identified in the literature, it is a minor theme in the Scottish data reported here.

In **Chapter** 5 it becomes apparent how the discourses of wellbeing described above play out in the context of education for social justice. Fielding (2007) describes how the functional and the personal aspects of schooling are deeply intertwined, and how different ideological approaches to education make us of this relationship. He makes a distinction between a neo-liberal 'high performance learning organisation' in which personal relationships and feelings are manipulated to be the servant of functional goals of performativity, and a welfare-liberal 'person centred learning community' in which learning is only undertaken if it is personally fulfilling and meaningful. I draw from Fielding's model to discuss how, in the high performance learning organisation, wellbeing, in the guise of social and emotional literacy may be fostered by a deliberative type of 'care' to foster the types of human capital favoured in the job market. Conversely, the 'person centred learning community' sees the functional aspect of schooling (learning) to be a truly caring activity which serves to enhance wellbeing as flourishing, and democratic fellowship. This model provides an analytical basis of the critical discourses analysis of Scottish policy that follows. However, unlike Fielding's work, this study is not seeking to compare schools, but rather is exploring discourses. It is not simply seeking to identify which of these discourses is in operation, but is instead looking to see where and how each of these is evident, and how they overlap.

Chapter 6 explores how wellbeing is conceptualised in Scottish education policy. Focussing on the health and wellbeing policies of 'Curriculum for Excellence' (Scottish Government n.d.-a, n.d.-b) and the partner interagency policy 'Getting it Right for Every Child' (Scottish Government 2012) it will be demonstrated that wellbeing is mainly characterised in terms of social and emotional literacy, linked to a discourse of care. The discourse of physical health is less prominent, but is a key theme. Analysis of these policies shows how childhood wellbeing is conceptualised in an individualised way, focusing inwardly as young people learn to manage themselves their emotions and behaviours in socially acceptable ways and to recognise and navigate risk.

The discourse of sustainability within the context of wellbeing is much quieter although, as an emerging discourse this may change in the near future. Most notably the discourse of flourishing through leading a valuable life is virtually absent in these papers. I will argue that wellbeing discourses of other professional groups have been adopted widely in education policy, overshadowing educational discourses and downplaying the contribution to wellbeing that can uniquely be made by teachers.

Chapter 7 continues to examine Scottish policy as it critically analyses the discursive relationships between wellbeing and learning. Repeatedly throughout the documents wellbeing is portrayed as a prerequisite to learning, and a support to the development of desired attitudes and dispositions. In particular it is depicted as the and the bedrock of the 'four capacities' which are the overarching aim of the 'Curriculum for Excellence'.[1] The wellbeing policy can also be explicitly linked to the economic policy. It is portrayed as a set of individualised skills which are servant to other purposes of education, rather than as an outcome of an enriched educational experience.

Overall the Scottish policy documentation invites an interpretation of a government attempt to appropriate the discourse of wellbeing to support a human capital project, in the model of the high performance learning organisation (Fielding 2007). Yet, there is a dissonance between this and the welfarist aspirations to which Scotland lays claim (Paterson 2003). An alternative interpretation is that of policy making as 'muddle'. Possibly, somehow, at the interagency discussion table the intrinsic value of education was simply overlooked as an aspect childhood flourishing, and the middle level bureaucrats who drafted the policies were unaware of the message they were sending. This may be an example of discourses acting behind the backs of the subjects.

Chapter 8 presents and examines interview data to show how the discourses of wellbeing articulated in policy are recontextualised by teachers and policy actors. It shows how the discourses are differently received by individuals, providing some insight as to the complexity involved in the way discourses move within a speech community. It demonstrates that the policy discourses have been naturalised in the speech of Scottish educators with many interviewees passively accepting and echoing the written policy. Others further entrenched the policy position of wellbeing as a servant to other purposes, by conflating the notion of wellbeing with successful learning, or by construing wellbeing as a solution to other problems. A minority of the interviewees drew from a wider understanding of their role as educator in identifying high quality teaching and learning as a key contribution to children's wellbeing as flourishing. These provide some detailed and helpful insights into how wellbeing in schools might be viewed in a more equitable and

[1]The 'four capacities' of the 'Curriculum for Excellence' are: successful learner, confident individual, effective contributor and responsible citizen.

way, that can be seen as recognising and supporting the diversity between children as they are encouraged to 'learn to be human'. This chapter also demonstrates the complexity of this topic as people could ascribe to several discourses simultaneously in the same interview, showing how deeply interwoven the different discourses of wellbeing have become.

In conclusion **Chap.** 9 synthesises the arguments developed throughout the book. Firstly, it discusses the potential hazards for social justice that can be enacted in the name of wellbeing when dominant discourses are uncritically accepted and children's emotions and characters are marshalled towards pre-determined goals. Secondly, and more positively, using the Capability Approach as a framework, it presents a more comprehensive view, showing how all of the discourses of wellbeing can be incorporated in a way that values the contribution that teachers, uniquely, make to the wellbeing of children, with inclusive approaches to teaching and learning enhancing all aspects of wellbeing in a way that enhances the freedoms of children and future adults to lead lives that they value.

This is followed by **Chap.** 10, "**appendix**" which outlines the methods used in the study.

Chapter 2
Discourse and Policy

The main purpose of this book is to explore the effects of the use of language, or discourse, relating to the school-based policies of wellbeing. In order to contextualise the analyses that appear later in the book, this chapter will introduce and discuss the concept of discourse, relating this to policy formation and its interpretation. What follows is a fairly generic introduction to discourse and policy, but for a reader who is unfamiliar with academic studies in these areas it is an important basis for understanding the arguments later in the book.

J. Spratt, *Wellbeing, Equity and Education*, Inclusive Learning and Educational Equity 1, DOI 10.1007/978-3-319-50066-9_2

Firstly, I will introduce the concept of discourse, examining what it is, and discussing the role of discourse in shaping behaviours. The role of discourse in masking dominant ideologies by naturalising ideas as 'common sense' will be discussed. I will explore the ways that powerful groups use discourse in policies that are designed to shape the behaviours of professionals towards particular goals. The discussion will move on to consider how policies are made and enacted, and how international ideological influences coalesce on educational and wellbeing policies. Finally, there is a short consideration of the nature and enactment of discourse analysis.

2.1 What Is Discourse?

Discourse can be seen as the use of language (spoken or written) by social actors in specific settings (Wodak 2008) and is the means by which people represent their view of the world (Fairclough 2003). However, people do not arrive at their world view in a vacuum; individuals are deeply embedded in social, cultural and historical contexts. Discourses are described as being both socially constructed and socially constitutive (Wodak 2009), in other words they emerge from the social action of groups of people, but at the same time they also mould the social world, shaping people's perceptions and behaviours. Hence the significance of discourse lies in its social function, and in the way in which power and control can be mediated through discourse.

To exemplify how discourse is both socially constructed and socially constitutive in education, I will digress briefly to consider the discourse of 'fixed ability labelling' and its twin concept of 'potential'. This view of learning, based on an assumption that 'intelligence' is innate, immutable, and normally distributed, emerged from a human invention, the Intelligence Quotient test, whose widespread use led to the construction of a discourse that remains prevalent today, in spite of searing critique (Gould 1996). It gave rise to the unquestioned categorisation of children using terms such as 'high ability' and 'low ability' coupled with deterministic assumptions about future achievements. The socially constitutive effects of the fixed ability discourse are evident in the systems and practices of contemporary schooling, such as setting, streaming and some forms of differentiation. These practices, it is argued, serve to lower teachers' expectations of children and undermine children's sense of self-worth, which in turn contributes to the reproduction social inequality (Hart 1998; Hart et al. 2004). This provides an example of the far-reaching effects that a dominant educational discourse can have on the lives of children, and in maintaining structural injustices in society.

However, although we can argue that discourse shapes the educational world, only some construals of the world have this constitutive power. Some discourses are privileged over others and the more powerful groups in society have greater access to platforms of public discourse (van Dijk 1997). Moreover, discourses do not only represent the world as it is seen to be in the present, they are also projective, and can represent possible worlds, thus can be used to bring about change. However, as Fairclough (2010, p. 5) comments, 'We cannot transform the world in any old way we happen to construe it; the world is such that only some transformations are possible'. The dominant discourses at the time will determine the direction of change. This is particularly important for this book which is exploring how the contemporary discourses of wellbeing in schools have been shaped.

In education, policy is an important public platform for the dissemination of discourse. Policies are produced by governments or other organisations of state, to purposefully influence the behaviour of citizens. According to Foucault, (1984, p. 123) 'Any system of education is a political way of maintaining or modifying the appropriation of discourses along with the knowledges and powers which they carry'. Thus, Ball (2008) argues that attention should be paid to the discourses of educational policies as these have a strong impact upon the construction of meaning, and consequently the relationships, imperatives and inevitabilities in schools. Arguably the social implications of the discourses associated with the 'wellbeing agenda' in schools have potentially far-reaching influences on the behaviour of teachers and, therefore, on the learning and development of children, and it is this that justifies such a close scrutiny of these emerging discourses.

Whilst writers may refer to 'dominant discourses', for example, currently we often can identify capitalist discourses as dominating discussions of globalisation, in fact multiple discourses can and do operate simultaneously. Jager and Maier (2009) present a view of discourse as a flow of knowledge that changes over time, which results in any number of competing societal discourses at any one moment in history, referring to a 'giant milling mass' of discourses. Not only do multiple discourses exist simultaneously, it is perfectly possible for competing discourses to be evident within the same institution (Rogers 2008) or for a single individual to ascribe to seemingly contradictory discourses (Fairclough 2003). One of the tasks of this book, is to disentangle the complex web of discourses which seem to converge around the concept of wellbeing.

2.2 How Discourse Works: Discourse and Ideology

Discourses are not simply random ways of talking. They are grounded in ideologies. Van Dijk (2006b) defines ideology as a belief system, which is socially shared by a group of people. Ideologies, he argues are a particularly fundamental, or seemingly axiomatic, type of belief, and are socially and politically important because they control and organise other types of beliefs, and the associated choices that people make. Ideological representations contribute to relationships of power and domination. For example, a racist ideology may control beliefs about immigration. Ideologies, therefore, specify the cultural values (for example understandings of freedom, equality and justice) which are relevant to a group. For example, in Chap. 3, I will discuss how neo-liberal and welfare liberal ideologies can be shown to give rise to contrasting understandings of the purposes of education and its role in social justice.

Ideology and discourse are closely related concepts, but not entirely congruent. Fairclough (2010) describes this as a dialectical relationship whereby one could not exist without the other, so ideology is part of discourse and discourse is part of ideology, but none the less they are distinguishable. Ideologies are shaped through the dominant discourses of powerful groups and vice versa. If power is seen as having control over the actions of other people then we can see that language can control people either through direct command, through persuasion, or through subtler use of discourse. Through their privileged access to platforms of public discourse, those in power can shape the intentions, actions and speech of individuals, to align with their own interests (van Dijk 1997). The makers of education policy hold a powerful position in terms of subtly moulding the beliefs and behaviours of teachers towards their own ideology. This has potentially far reaching effects on many aspects of the lives of children.

However, individuals may not be fully aware of the ideologies to which they ascribe and which are represented through their discursive actions. Fairclough (2010) argues that interactions such as conversations depend upon taken for granted assumptions or background knowledge, which serves to naturalise ideological representations so that they appear as 'common sense' rather than ideology. By taking on the mantle of common sense the ideology becomes opaque to the participants. In this vein Wodak and Meyer (2009) describe naturalised discourse as a form of collusion, suggesting that ideologies are transmitted 'behind the back of the subject, while the actors do not understand the game' (p. 17). Those educational policies that are most successful are those whose discourses become naturalised within the 'speech communities' of schools. This book will argue that the concept of wellbeing has been naturalised in schools, to become part of everyday, taken for granted speech, with little scrutiny.

When a particular ideology has become naturalised within the population a situation of hegemony is reached (ibid). According to van Dijk (1997) hegemonic power causes people to act as if their choices were natural, made of free will and in such a situation commands and coercion by the dominant groups are not required. Expressions such as the 'wellbeing agenda' or the 'wellbeing movement' (Layard 2011) suggest that the acceptance of public interventions in personal wellbeing may be becoming hegemonic. Yet, as will be shown, the language of wellbeing can be put to work to support different ideological positions.

2.3 Different Schools of Thought in Studies of Discourse

It should be noted that there are different schools of thought about the relationship between individual actors and their use of discursive practices. There is a divide in the literature between a post-structural view of discourse stemming from European philosophy and cultural thought, and a linguistic view of discourse which is Anglo-American in origin (MacLure 2003). The post-structural approach does not view people as rational self-aware individuals, but instead believes that people's identities are formed by the discourses to which they are exposed (Foucault 1973). This approach holds that there is no social reality other than discourse. From a Foucauldian perspective, it is not the subject who produces the discourse, but the discourse which produces the subject (Jager and Maier 2009). The post-structural view is not so much concerned with close analysis of texts, but with the use of discursive practices operating at a social level. In this view, truths are always partial and knowledge always 'situated'.

However, other writers pay more attention to the role that individuals play in interpreting discourses in the light of their own experiences. Van Dijk (2006a) argues that if ideology is a belief system, then there must be a role for cognition in an individual's development of belief. He refers to the 'mental maps' or 'context maps' that people create in order to interpret their experiences in the context of their understandings of the social world. This has been supported empirically by numerous research studies which identify the role of individuals in interpreting and enacting policy discourses (e.g. Evans et al. 2013; Maguire et al. 2015; Pickard 2010; Grue 2009).

In this book I take a view that what is said and what it is possible to say are, to some extent, moderated by the cognitive processes and active choices of individuals, albeit deeply influenced by the dominant discourses. Instead of taking a post-structural view this work leans more towards an understanding of discourse as a linguistic practice. However, the main interest is not linguistics per se, but in the social impact of the discourses which are expressed. Therefore, the work will draw from the field of Critical Discourse Analysis (CDA), which is based on an assumption that use of language is closely related to other aspects of social life. Its origins lie in 'critical linguistics' a branch of linguistics which developed in the 1970s (van Leeuwen 2009). It offers an approach to discourse analysis which is interested in the use of language, primarily for its social effects (Fairclough 2003).

Whilst acknowledging the post-structural argument about the conditional nature of 'truth' and the contextual influences on 'knowledge', in this book I take a realist stance. This is a position which believes that social and political structures and forces do exist, although they may be differently understood and not always easy to identify (Fairclough 2010). For example, it may be unclear exactly how social forces work to create the conditions of poverty that disproportionately affect certain groups of people, but it is factually true that this happens. Furthermore, the limitations that poverty places on the lives of individuals are very real, albeit differently experienced.

2.4 Discourse and Policy

Government policy is an important platform for gaining power over discourses. School based policies, such as the wellbeing policies are designed to shape discourses and alter the behaviour of teachers and other professionals in school.

This section will consider the process of policy of formulation and enactment, and consider the role of discourse within this process.

Social policy can be seen as actions and positions taken by the state (which consists of a range of institutions), in order to steer the actions of citizens (Rizvi and Lingard 2010), and is a form of discursive action. According to Ball (2008) a contemporary account of education should also acknowledge the role of the business sector in shaping the direction of policy, thereby identifying a route through which new discourses, and new forms of regulation are migrating into education policy.

However, policy is more than simply documentation, or actions of those in positions of authority. Policy is a process, which includes influence, policy production, textual expressions of policy and implementation. Thus policy has been characterised as 'text and action, words and deeds' and 'what is enacted as well as what is intended' (Ball 1994, cited in Rizvi and Lingard 2010). Viewed in this way, it is clear that policy is not absolute, (despite the appearance of the documentation), but is subject to negotiation, struggle and compromise in its design and open to interpretation, by social actors, during its implementation (Ozga 2000).

One facet of policy is the documentation produced by government departments in order to express and disseminate their position. According to Lingard and Ozga (2007), the field of education policy includes all texts seeking to influence educational practices, with the exception of curricula. Rather oddly, they state that curriculum and pedagogy are 'constituted as intellectual fields outside the purview of education policy' (p. 2). Whilst this may have been true in 1976 when the, then, prime minister Jim Callaghan famously referred to the curriculum as a 'secret garden' in his Ruskin College speech, from this point onwards government intervention in all aspects of schooling has become the norm across the UK (Chitty 2009) including the implementation of national curricula. Ball's (2007) suggestion that policy shapes what it means to be educated and what it means to learn would seems to be a better representation of the contemporary position. Scotland's 'Curriculum for Excellence', (Education Scotland undated) and the New Zealand Curriculum (Ministry of Education 2007), to name just two, provide a clear examples of the way twenty-first century governments have drawn curriculum and pedagogy into the work of policy.

It is worth taking a moment to consider the processes by which policy is produced. Contemporary accounts of the policy process dismiss models which view it as a step-wise, linear and logical series of stages flowing from evidence gathering to policy formulation, to documentation then implementation (e.g. John 1998; Hudson and Lowe 2009). Rizvi and Lingard (2010) suggest this is due to changes in the social sciences, such as the discrediting of the positivist models of research on which this process was predicated, the emergence of new theoretical developments such as post-structuralism, feminism and critical theory, the loss of popularity of Keynesian economic theories on which many policies were based, and most significantly, they suggest, influences of globalised capitalism.

However, whilst all of these factors may be significant, a widely quoted paper debunking the notion of rationalist policy making was published well in advance of these developments. In *The science of "muddling through"* Lindblom (1959) discussed the complexity of policy making, such as the wide range of goals that may be addressed in a single policy, the plurality of interests that may be attended to, and the limited evidence that may be available to inform the decision making process. He suggested that a 'good' policy was often one which interested parties agreed on, even if none thought it best met their particular goals. He used the phrase 'muddling through' to capture this procedure, suggesting that it could either be portrayed as a sophisticated process of complex decision making or, alternatively, as no process at all. More recently the term 'muddle' is widely adopted to describe policy development (e.g. (John 1998, e.g. Hudson and Lowe 2009), often paying little heed to the original article which portrayed 'muddling through' as a difficult and complex, (if somewhat haphazard) process, rather than simply an incompetent mess.

So, from inception, through design and delivery we can see a messy process of working and reworking, argument, compromise and perhaps 'fudge'. Yet, the outcomes of this process are powerful discourses which impact very directly on the lives of citizens. More recent accounts of policy making echo Lindblom's ideas, suggesting that policies are usually heteroglossic in nature in order to appease a wide range of interests. Education policy may interact with other policies, in fields such as such as economics or health. Policy readership is much wider than the practitioners who may enact it, and therefore policy may seek to suture different, even oppositional ideological positions (Rizvi and Lingard 2010). Thus Ball (2007) describes policy making as a process of 'bricolage' whereby bits and pieces are borrowed, copied, and amended from elsewhere, resulting in policies which may appear incoherent. This, of course makes the task of the policy analyst rather complex, since rarely do a cogent set of theoretical or political principles translate unabridged into policy, even where dominant influences may be evident (Ball ibid).

Policy is increasingly shaped by international influences. Not only do policy makers borrow and abridge ideas from colleagues world-wide, they are deeply influenced by pressures of globalisation, much of which is economic. Although the term globalisation suggests that governments around the world are facing similar pressures, it is increasingly recognised that they do not necessarily respond in the same way. Each nation must mediate the global influences within its own historical and cultural context (Hudson and Lowe 2009). Ozga and Lingard (2007) refer to the local response to international pressures as the vernacular. In this vein, Winter (2012) describes 'vernacular globalisation' as the constitution of 'hybrid education policies' through the combined effect of the global policy discourses and the historical cultural and political narratives in the national policy arena. In contemporary Scottish policy the neo-liberal discourses of economic ambition are in tension with a long standing national tradition of social democracy national (Paterson 2003) with a government that seeks to build a nation which is both 'wealthier' and 'fairer' (Scottish Government 2011).

An important aspect of policy formation is the choice of language that is used, in order to appeal to the readers and users of the document. Contemporary policies tend to use a limited vocabulary of carefully chosen key terms which repeat throughout the document, with the intention that these will become the naturalised forms of reference. The erstwhile Secretary of State for Education in England, Gillian Shephard, is quoted by Atkins and Wallace (2012) as saying, 'We [government] must emphasise words that people find attractive.' Hence, one of the strategies of policy making is to lexicalise in ways that appear uncontroversial and appeal to 'common sense'. One of the main arguments of this book is that the concept of 'wellbeing' has been chosen as a policy focus precisely because of its widespread attractiveness, (who could be opposed to childhood wellbeing?) yet close scrutiny of policies reveals that it can be used to serve agendas that may be less 'soft and cuddly' than the vocabulary implies.

Similarly, the implementation stage of policy is not straightforward. As Ozga (2000) noted, policy is rarely delivered to a grateful or quiescent population, but it is interrogated, interpreted, remodelled and delivered in the cultural and personal contexts of the organisations and individuals involved. According to Bernstein (2000) policy is recontextualised as it moves between its production phase and its implementation phase, and the interpretation by practitioners is a point at which new discourses can emerge, and in this 'discursive gap' alternative possibilities exist. As education policies arrive at the implementation phase they are translated by professionals through a process of decoding and recoding, at which point individuals bring their own moral frameworks to bear (Singh et al. 2013). This was clearly demonstrated in a study which showed how health imperatives relating to diet exercise and weight, were 'performed' differently as they were reassembled in the unique cultural and relational context of each school (Evans et al. 2013). In this way, the workers, are not simply the vehicles of delivery, but can be seen as active makers of policy (Maguire et al. 2015). Thus, it is clear that the intentions of policies in the production stage do not necessarily tally with outcomes in the implementation phase. For this reason, research into education policy can be enhanced by examining how it is received by teachers.

2.5 Discourse Analysis

Discourse analysis has been likened to a puzzle (van Leeuwen 2009) which is addressed by looking at the statements that are dispersed and repeated in different contexts. Discourse analysis is based mainly on texts, which can include written documents, transcripts of spoken language, such as interview transcripts, TV or radio broadcasts etc. However, Wodak (2009) reminds us also, where appropriate to take account of other forms of semiotic communication including images and iconography.

One of the key principles of discourse analysis is the study of recontextualisation (Bernstein 1990). This refers to the way in which discourses change as they move between different groups. For example, when teachers read and interpret written policies there may be a shift in the way in which the topic is understood. By observing how discourses cross refer to each other we can see how they transfer between contexts. By looking for links between the discourses in different contexts (intertextuality) we can see people draw from other texts either explicitly or implicitly to justify the positions that they hold (Fairclough 2003). We can also see how discourses are changed as they flow between different speech communities.

Jager and Maier (2009) suggest that flows of discourse that centre on a common topic, can be grouped and sub-grouped into smaller topics. This is one of the approaches adopted in this project, as it seeks to identify different themes that coalesce around the notion of wellbeing in the school context. Discursive themes of wellbeing as emotional and social literacy, wellbeing as physical health promotion, wellbeing as care, wellbeing as flourishing and wellbeing as sustainability will be identified and explored. Interestingly, Jager and Maier (ibid) discuss how entanglements of discourses can occur where one text addresses several topics, and moreover a single statement can involve an entanglement of discourses (a discursive 'knot'). Again, this project shows how different representations of the concept of wellbeing have become entangled with each other. One of the tasks of this work is to begin to tease out the different discourses.

Discourse analysis is used in research for different purposes. In some cases, the goals of discourse analysis may be simply descriptive, seeking to offer an account of what has been said without offering an explanation, or it may uncritically accept the assumptions in the text. However, Critical Discourse Analysis (CDA) is an approach which deliberately seeks to unmask ideologies and reveal the power relations at play behind the veneer of 'common sense'. CDA distinguishes itself from other types of discourse analysis by the requirement of criticality. This implies a normative element to the analysis, i.e. that the discourses are analysed in reference to a set of values, identifying where those values are, or are not, adhered to (Fairclough 2010). Thus the analysis will examine the ways in which ideologies are justified and propagated, and will demonstrate how linguistic strategies serve to make some positions seem more rational than others, and will identify inconsistencies and contradictions within and between texts.

Social power (as opposed to individual power that may exist in a one-to-one relationship) is an important concept in CDA, as it is through the dominant discourses of powerful groups that ideologies are shaped. CDA plays an active role in exposing the power structures which give rise to inequality. This is a repeating theme in the literature, and to some is seen as an underpinning principle of CDA. For example, van Leeuwen (2009) claims that critical discourse analysts are united by a common goal, 'the critique of dominant discourse and genres that effect inequalities, injustices and oppression in contemporary society' (p. 278). Similarly, van Dijk (1993) states that CDA focuses on the 'role of discourse in the (re)production and challenge of dominance' (p. 249). A number of the key writers in this field have devoted their work to the challenge of particular discourses that create inequality, notably Wodak's work on racist discourses and Fairclough's critique of neo-liberal discourse of globalisation. However, Rogers (2008) cautions that over ardent pursuit of a particular discursive stance, without proper analysis can result in work which is political rather than researcherly.

In addition to critiquing how well-established discourses exert power and create hegemony, CDA has a role in examining emerging discourses, to explore how existing discourses can be conflated, or how one discursive strand can outcompete another as new discourses emerge. The ‘wellbeing agenda’ is still a fairly new initiative, at least in formal policy, and there are a number of discourses which coalesce in this area. Jager and Maier (2009) suggest that the role of CDA is to disentangle the ‘milling mass’ of discourses through a critical lens. Rather than focussing on unmasking a single ideology, this book will examine the influences of and interplay between two ideologies which are often in tension in the educational world: that of neo-liberalism and welfare liberalism, to explore how each of these are played out through the discourses of wellbeing as they appear in schools. This is not an attempt to dichotomise the discourses as either neo-liberalism of welfare liberalism, it is a more nuanced exploration of how these different ideologies bump along together in the complex reality of education. The book will show how the concept of wellbeing can be put to different ideological purposes, and how the vagueness of the concept of wellbeing can allow these to be conflated. Moreover, it will show how discourses of wellbeing support different understandings of equity and social justice. This is clearly a policy field which has considerable impact upon the educational and developmental experiences of children, an issue in which power and control are never far away.

2.5.1 The Role of the Researcher in Discourse Analysis

An important point to note in conducting discourse a Critical Discourse Analysis, is that the being a researcher does not place somebody outside of discourse. As human beings the analysts are just as embroiled in discourses as anybody else. For this reason, Jager and Maier (2009) caution the analyst to recognise his /her own position within the ‘milling mass’ and to state that position clearly.

My own position, as a life-long educationalist, lies with a firm belief in education as a serving the personal development of individuals, so that children can lead fulfilling lives in the present and in the future. Like many other educationalists I believe a view of schooling as simply serving economic purposes is an impoverishment of learning. However, I would not ignore the role of schooling in preparing young people for useful employment. Whilst not viewing economic activity as the only way to judge the quality of a life, I would acknowledge that income generation allows wider choices in how a person lives, and conversely poverty can stifle opportunities to be happy. I would also see fulfilling employment as potentially life-enhancing, and that schooling has a role to play in preparing young people for good employment opportunities.

However, I am opposed to practices which deliberately shape young people’s characters or subjectivities solely for the purposes of enhancing their economic potential. In this book, one of the things that will be ‘unmasked’ is the way in which seemingly benign discourses of wellbeing can be put to purposes of human capital creation.

2.6 Summary

The notion of discourse has been introduced as the means by which people represent their view of the world. Discourse is seen as both socially constructed and socially constitutive. Discourses are the means by which powerful groups exert influence in society, and the way in which dominant ideologies are propagated. Yet the speaker may be unaware of the ideologies that they espouse, when they adopt 'common sense' language that has been naturalised in everyday speech. Multiple discourses may operate at the same time (as is the case with wellbeing) and become entangled with each other.

Education policy is discussed as a platform through which those in power can influence the discursive actions, and the behaviours of teachers and other professionals in schools. International influence on educational policies include both neoliberal policies and more welfarist, child centred policies. It is clear that there are powerful and competing influences on policy that can have far reaching effects on the experiences of children. This chapter has provided a platform for the discussions of educational policies of wellbeing that follow.

Chapter 3
Equity, Schooling and Wellbeing

Debates about how to address to inequalities in children's lives often focus on wellbeing (e.g. McLaughlin 2015). This book will explore how the concept of wellbeing is utilised in educational contexts, and will identify the significance of this for discussions of equity and social justice. In this chapter I will start developing the argument by considering the purposes of education, and how we understand equity in schooling. In a discussion about justice in the school setting, we need to understand what we are trying to fair about and what we mean by equality.

J. Spratt, *Wellbeing, Equity and Education*, Inclusive Learning and Educational Equity 1, DOI 10.1007/978-3-319-50066-9_3

3.1 Equality of What?

The question 'Equality of what' was posed by the philosopher and economist Amartya Sen (1992), whose work discussed the problem of fair distribution of resources, in a world where people are all different. Within any system that claims to be egalitarian, Sen argues, some 'focal variables' are endorsed, while others are rejected. Focal variables could include any aspect by which people can be compared, for example, income, wealth, happiness, quality of life, opportunities, rights or educational outcomes. In a theoretical world in which equity was seen as equal incomes for everybody, this would not provide equivalent qualities of life, as some people have greater needs. For example, travelling is more expensive for wheelchair users. This simple example demonstrates that equality in one focal variable (income) may result in inequality in another (opportunities to travel freely). It also demonstrates that some people are more readily able to convert one resource (income) into another valuable activity (travel). Similarly, in the context of schooling, for a wide range of reasons, some children can more readily convert educational resources (such as literacy lessons) into activities (such as reading for enjoyment) (Maddox 2008). Therefore, it is important to consider the metaphorical space in which we make judgements about equality.

Two key points can be drawn from these examples. Firstly, that when trying to be equitable we need to consider what we are trying to achieve. Therefore, in addressing issues of justice in education, we need to ask what is education for? Secondly, the wide diversity of human circumstances means that 'equal treatment for all may demand very unequal treatment in favour of the disadvantaged' (Sen 1992, p. 1). Human beings are thoroughly diverse in terms of personal factors (such as gender, age, ethnicity, (dis)abilities,) as well as external factors (such as wealth, poverty, environmental conditions, social conditions). Any consideration of equality should take account of the fundamental differences between people. Equality is not reached by treating everybody the same.

The following sections will consider the question 'equality of what?' in relation to schooling. If we are aiming to provide an equitable educational experience to all, we need to examine the purpose(s) of education and the nature of justice within the education system. In the section that follows I will discuss how liberal understandings of education have diverged, giving rise to seemingly opposing ideologies, of welfare liberalism and neo-liberalism, each ascribing a different purpose to education and a different approach to social justice. Later I will suggest that, in reality, there may not be an absolute dichotomy of understandings, but that education may be seen to have composite purposes, drawing from different understandings of social justice.

3.2 Liberal Ideologies in Education

The word liberal is used to convey different meanings. In philosophy, it is used to denote a well-established tradition that values freedom, whereas in political usage it has been adopted in ways which convey both left wing and right wing connotations (Robeyns 2005). This section will show how classical liberalism has evolved divergently to give rise to the two philosophically and politically distinct ideologies of welfare liberalism and neo-liberalism (or free-market liberalism), and comment on how justice is conceptualised in each. It will then examine the demands made of education by each stance.

The concept of 'ideology' is fundamental to Critical Discourse Analysis. This was examined in detail in Chap. 2, where I discussed how ideologies shape the discourses that are 'taken for granted' in everyday speech. The discussion of liberal ideologies below will underpin much of the subsequent analysis of the discourses of wellbeing in schooling.

3.2.1 Classical Liberalism

The classical liberal model of governance gained currency at the end of feudalism when the notion of the individual as an autonomous political entity first emerged (Olssen et al. 2004). Classical liberalism constructed the notion of the private sphere existing around individuals, allowing them to follow their interests without interference from the state, (Brighouse and Unterhalter 2010) or coercion from other citizens (Plant 2010). Freedom, in this view is a negative concept, i.e. freedom from interference. A key concept in classical liberal theory is Aristotle's (1985) notion of the 'good life', or human flourishing (eudaimonia). Liberal justice required that citizens were free to develop their own conception of 'the good' and to pursue it. The purpose of education was, therefore, to enhance the capacity of the individual to become a rational autonomous citizen, able to identify and appreciate whatever, for him (at this time only men could be citizens), was the good (Arneil 2002).

However, classical liberalism did not only promote self-interest. Brighouse (2000) argues that an important aspect of 'the good' was concern for others, and contributions to civil society. Yet, classical liberalism put no compulsion on wealthy individuals to contribute to philanthropic activities if they chose not to, and moreover, left the decisions about how any such charity should be directed in the hands of the rich. The 'justice' afforded through the system of classical liberalism enhanced the freedoms of those with the resources to benefit from education and to pursue the 'good' life unimpeded by the state, but it was deeply unjust to women, and to poorer people who were denied the status of citizenship (Apple 2006). The following sections show how more modern concepts of liberalism have drawn from different aspects of classical liberalism to divergently evolve into 'welfare liberalism' and 'neo-liberalism'.

3.2.2 Welfare Liberalism

The industrial revolution brought demand for an infrastructure, funded through taxation, and henceforth the state took a more interventionist role in the lives of individuals through provision of public goods and services. Notions of social democracy, enhanced opportunity and redistribution of wealth to some extent underpinned these policies. Whilst a focus on individual freedom was maintained, it was extended to embrace positive freedom as the state was enhancing the options and choices available to the general population (Olssen et al. 2004). Universal education played an important role in widening opportunities for poorer people. Although the state was playing a much larger role in structuring and supporting individual lives, this was achieved in a way that was seen as congruent with ideals of individual freedom and hence this has been referred to as welfare-liberalism (Olssen et al. *ibid*).

In the welfare liberalist ideology, the primary purpose of education continued to be to develop the capacities of individuals to lead lives that they value. This, in turn, was seen to be beneficial to the development and sustainability of communities and to serve to strengthen democratic fellowship. Education was also seen to have a role in integrating society in terms of gender, class and ethnicity. Thus welfare liberalism views every individual as important, but acknowledges that people benefit from their associations with others, and that communities are strengthened by the skills, talents and wellbeing of the individual citizens (Brighouse 2000), thus creating a form of 'thick democracy' (Apple 2006).

3.2.3 Neo-liberalism

Towards the end of the 20th century neo-liberal ideas gained political currency in the English speaking world. Robert Nozick's (1974) influential work *Anarchy, State and Utopia* argued for 'separateness of persons', recognising only atomised individuals, and rejecting any notions of society. Nozick held an 'entitlement' view of justice, that each individual deserved whatever resources he or she was able to legally gain through free and unfettered exchange. Therefore, for him, justice was achieved by removing restrictive conditions that may inhibit individual freedom, and minimising redistribution of resources within society. In the neo-liberal view, political freedom is closely allied with economic freedom (Plant 2010).

Nozick's ideas share many of the characteristics of classical liberalism, such as individualism and a focus on negative freedoms. A reduction of state intervention and a flexible deregulated labour market are seen to offer opportunities to individuals to maximise their own potential. Citizens are recognised mainly in terms of their economic activities, and public services are marketised, giving rise to a form of 'thin democracy' predicated on choice (Apple 2006). Linked to shifts from 'Fordist' economies of mass industrial production to the 'knowledge based' economic systems (Ball 2007), the ideas of neo-liberalism gained currency in UK and USA policy in the 1990s. However, although neo-liberalism reduces bureaucracy, unlike classical liberalism, it does not relinquish control (Olssen et al. 2004). Neo-liberalism shifted to laissez-faire politics whilst simultaneously introducing new forms of governance (Winter 2012).

Neoliberalism views education as a commodity to be traded in the job-market, and therefore a personal benefit, but also of critical value to the national interest as countries vie for position in the international economy. In this model, the public 'good' delivered by education is not strong community relationships or local solidarity; rather it is the opposite. By encouraging competition between individuals, each seeking to outperform each other, the overall aim is to augment the national bank of human capital, enhancing efficiency and profitability in international markets. Successful neo-liberalism requires a very particular sort of autonomous and self-reliant subject (Fielding 2011). Increasingly, the understanding of human capital is being extended from knowledge and skills to personal attributes, competences, and attitudes. As the notion of human capital extends its reach to very personal aspects of being, concepts such as 'resilience', and self-efficacy' (often badged as 'wellbeing') gain currency and education is drawn centre stage in creating what Gillies (2011) calls 'high yield citizens'.

To ensure that schools subscribe to this model, methods of persuasion must be in place. Ball (2007) writes about the ways in which the control of schools in England has combined the methods of the free market, with new systems of governance. He describes how policies have led to new forms of state 'steering', with an emphasis on accountability to targets. Autonomous school management, parental choice and elements of selection have led to market-place competition between schools. Whilst state intervention is minimal in the day to day running of institutions, schools are judged on their outcomes, against government targets, and those schools which are successful attract more students and hence more funding, whilst those which fail face penalties. Writing in the USA, Apple (2006) identifies the role of a new stratum of bureaucracy, the 'professional and managerial new middle class', whose role is to draft the policies, to design and implement the mechanisms of measurement to serve the new styles of governance.[1] Such a performativity approach to regulation, Ball (2003) suggests is a neo-liberal model relying on markets to drive up standards, whilst simultaneously maintaining control through systems of monitoring.

If education is thought to be a commodity that can be traded in the job-market, then worthwhile knowledge enhances human capital and the value of education is judged in terms of it marketability. Arising from this stance is a model of social justice in which fairness is associated with measurable educational outcomes, employability and potential generation of income. Instead of intervention in the market place, this approach would address issues of equality by attempting to

[1]Apple (2006) points out that many of the individuals who take on these roles may very see themselves as politically left-leaning, having devoted their lives to public service, yet in the name of 'efficiency' they design and implement the instruments of the capitalist state.

support individuals to be able to cope in the competitive job market (Leggett 2005). However, within this model of equity through accountability, arguments about social justice can be distorted by the way that statistics are analysed and presented. For example, in Ontario, Canada, a model of analysis that focussed on the differential attainment between boys and girls occluded information about other axes of inequality such as race or class (Rezai-Rashti et al. 2016). This returns us to Sen's (1992) argument that equality in one focal variable will result in inequality in another, so as educationalists must consider how we make judgements about equality.

3.2.4 Ideologies of Welfare Liberalism and Neo-liberalism – Summary

In summary, neo-liberalism and welfare liberalism share a common root in classical liberalism. Neo-liberalism is characterised by ontological individualism and self-interest, harnessed to fuel national economic success, whereas welfare liberalism values individual freedom to choose a life of value, whilst also viewing people as co-operative and interdependent. Whereas neo-liberalism sees education as an individual good and knowledge as a form of human capital, welfare liberalism sees education as both a public and a private good, having broad individual benefits, whilst enhancing the social and democratic fabric of society. For neo-liberalism social justice lies solely in providing opportunities to compete in the job market, whereas welfare liberalism sees social justice in expanding opportunities to lead a valuable life, in the context of a co-operative democratic society. Neoliberalism offers a form of 'thin democracy' based on economic freedom and choice, whereas welfare liberalism espouses 'thick democracy' based social solidarity, civic engagement and mutual responsibilities.

3.3 International Influences on Policy

Contemporary writers on education policy emphasise the importance of global influences on national policies, often linking this to the efforts made by nation states to vie for economic advantage. Discussions of internationalisation in education tend to focus on the neo-liberal ideology emanating from the USA (Rizvi 2004). International Organisations, particularly the World Bank, the United Nations Educational, Scientific and Cultural Organisation (UNESCO) and the Organisation for Economic Co-operation and Development (OECD) are seen as key influences behind a world culture which views education as an economic driver (Resnik 2006). Whilst these organisations have no direct control over the policies of nation states, Rutkowski (2007) argues that they use strategies to bring about 'soft convergence' of international educational policies. Such strategies include: creating of multilateral spaces for 'soft' laws to be formed[2]; implementation of policies through grants and loans; creating spaces in which multilateral policies can be created and exchanged; and becoming experts in measuring and evaluating education policy. One highly visible example of an international organisation exerting influence through its activities as expert evaluator is the OECD's international comparison of educational performance conducted by the Programme for International Student Assessment (PISA). The importance attached to PISA scores, it is claimed, have led to a global convergence of policy processes directed towards its educational indicators (Grek 2009), as countries seek competitive advantage in the international 'audit culture' (Kamens 2013).

The PISA scores are orientated towards those aspects of education that are deemed to be most economically advantageous, and hence Sellar and Lingard (2013) argue that 'PISA provides a measure of human capital flow into economies'. Moreover, increasingly PISA not only measures learning outcomes such as literacy and numeracy, it records attributes and capacities that may enhance business profitability such as motivation to learn, or learning strategies (Grek 2009). Plans exist to introduce the recording of 'collaborative problem solving', thereby extending its scope to interpersonal skills (Sellar and Lingard 2013). Education for human capital not only seeks to shape what children know, but also who they are (ibid), taking a future orientated interest in the skills and dispositions they will bring to the workforce as adults.

Whilst the main focus of the critique of international trends in education policy tends to fall on the marketization of education, we should not ignore the existence of other global influences on schooling, particularly in relation to childhood wellbeing. For example, the United Nations Convention of the Rights of the Child (United Nations 1989), is a powerful policy lever, whose purpose is to secure for children the level of care that would engender a childhood lived 'in the spirit of peace, dignity, tolerance, freedom, equality and solidarity' (p. 2), delivered through the framework of rights to provision, protection and participation. The World Health Organisation's Global Schools Health Initiative, calling for all schools to be 'health promoting' (World Health Organisation 1998) offers another example of global influence upon schooling which offers an alternative to the human capital discourse described above. A comparative report by UNICEF (2007) showing that UK children held the lowest overall ranking for wellbeing of all OECD countries, also sparked a flurry of policy activity across the UK (More recently the UK ranking has been revised upwards (UNICEF Office of Research 2013)). Whilst the term 'globalisation' is often understood as an overwhelmingly market driven influence on public policy, it should be noted that some significant international influences on education take a more childhood centred stance.

[2]'Soft' laws are international treaties, which may be, in theory, legally binding, but whose main influence is exerted as a tool for applying diplomatic and moral pressure on governments.

Moreover, as noted previously, individual countries respond to international pressures in different ways, that take into account the country's own history and sense of identity. Scotland's dual commitment to social justice and international competitiveness provide the political context for its vernacular education policies. The education policy from age 3–18 is articulated in the 'Curriculum for Excellence' (Education Scotland undated) which asserts an overarching aim that children and young people should develop the 'four capacities', namely 'successful learner', 'confident individual', 'responsible citizen' and 'effective contributor'. Commentators have both applauded these capacities as a welcome, (if somewhat incoherent), respite from an earlier target driven curriculum (Priestley 2010) and criticised them as overt bid to develop human capital (Lingard 2008), demonstrating the complexity and ambiguity of the purposes of the curriculum. It is not always easy to know the ideological intentions of the government. Readers from other countries may not be familiar with the specifics of Scottish policy, but will no doubt recognise the tensions that exist between different drivers of education in their own context.

3.4 The Multiple Purposes of Schooling

The previous section has outlined two seemingly oppositional ideologies that inform education and education policy. In analysing political and policy discourses in education it is important to be able to distinguish these schools of thought. However, if we stay with this dichotomy we start asking simple questions like: Does education serve economic purposes or does it serve to enhance personal freedom? Whereas, the more complex question is: How do these facets of education interact? This section explores the ways in which some educationalists have sought to reconcile these different standpoints, seeing education as having multiple purposes. At the same time, it is clear that tensions exist between the purposes, and that problems emerge when the economic targets of education are allowed to overshadow other aims.

Rather than seeing the different purposes of education as contradictory, Biesta (2010) argued that education has composite purposes. He suggested three different, related functions of education: qualification (skills, knowledge and dispositions that allow a person to *do* something), socialisation (teaching individuals how to adopt existing norms, values and ways of doing things) and subjectification (providing opportunities for unique qualities of individuals to come 'into presence', p. 80). Socialisation and subjectification are seen to be the opposite of each other, as socialisation is guiding children towards similar traits, so they can 'fit in' to contemporary society, whereas subjectification values and fosters the individuality of children. Whilst Biesta (ibid) acknowledged that one function of schooling is to teach children how to do the kind of things that may help them in securing employment (qualification), and, in a neo-liberal context this may involve a strong element of socialisation (in the development of personality traits that convert to human capital), he also stated that an education that socialises without also fostering subjectification is anti-educational. Thus the economic role of schooling is not ignored but, nor is it seen to trump the development of the individual person.

Similarly, Macmurray (2012), who saw the purpose of education as 'learning to be human', identified three priorities in education. The first priority is learning to live in personal relations, or learning to live in community. The second priority is 'education for sensibility' or the development of the capacity for sense experience, involving education of the emotions through arts, music and so on. The third priority, he called 'technological', and refers to acquiring techniques, either practical or intellectual, which have direct applications. The third priority, which to a great extent is preparation for the workplace, was, in Macmurray's view necessary, but is generally given too much emphasis in education. Where it is overemphasised, he argued the other two priorities are overshadowed, or even impeded, resulting in education failing in its true purpose of 'learning to be human'. Again we see an understanding of education that does not deny the economic purposes of education, but makes a claim for this to be one part of education that serves the development of, what Giovanola (2005) calls 'personhood and human richness'.

3.5 Equality of What? The Capability Approach

This chapter started with Sen's (1992) question, and it seems fitting to end by considering how he answered this himself, and introducing some key concepts that will inform the later arguments in this book. In addressing this question, Sen developed the Capability Approach to social justice. As outlined earlier, a basic premise of his work was that human diversity must be accounted for in any considerations of equality. Sen proposed that equality should be evaluated in terms of individual freedoms for people to lead lives that they have reason to value. Public policy, in this view, should seek to remove 'unfreedoms' such as poverty, or poor health care which restrict people's opportunities to pursue lives that they value. It should also take positive steps to enhance the opportunities available to people, and here we can see a key role for education. Sen coined the term Capability to refer to the freedom that a person has to choose a life that they have reason to value. It is not what a person does that is important – it is the range of things that they could choose to do. Human agency in choosing from a range of possibilities is a key concept in the Capability Approach, and the wider the range of possibilities, the greater an individual's Capability.

Opportunities to lead a valuable life can be assessed in terms of a person's 'functionings', i.e. what people do and who they are, described as their 'beings and doings'. The wider the range of possible functionings (not actual functionings), the more enhanced their Capability. Functionings may include learned skills such as literacy and numeracy, or states of being such as good health or freedom from disease. Equally they may include social opportunities such as democratic citizenship or membership of a particular social group, or emotional capacities such as empathy. It is a deliberately wide-ranging term, allowing for individual difference in what is viewed as an important functioning.

The term 'Capability'[3] is used to describe the opportunities that an individual has to develop valuable functionings. For Sen, the important point about equality is the freedoms available to people regardless of whether they take advantage of those opportunities. To illustrate the distinction between a capability and a functioning, Sen (2009), classically, gives the example of two people who are starving, both of whom would be seen as lacking the functioning of good physical health. However, one of those people has no food because of famine in the local area, whilst the other person is on hunger strike, as a political protest. Whilst the functioning of the two people is the same, their capabilities are completely different, as the hunger striker has the freedom to choose to eat, whilst the famine victim does not. A just society, in his view, would distribute its resources to enhance individual freedoms to pursue a life of value. This redistribution would take account of the different freedoms, or 'unfreedoms' that already existed, and the capacity of individuals to convert resources into valued activities.

Five types of 'instrumental freedoms' are identified in the Capability Approach (Sen 1995). These are basic conditions that contribute to overall Capability. These are defined as:

- Political freedom (e.g. democracy, right to free speech)
- Economic freedom (opportunities to earn and spend money)
- Social opportunities (e.g. education, health care, social care)
- Transparency guarantees
- Protective security (e.g. fair and just legal system, police force)

Beyond this, Sen demurred from listing what he thought were core capabilities, as he argued that individuals must ultimately make the choices about what is deemed to be valuable in their lives.

The focus of the Capability Approach, then, is on expanding freedoms of individuals so they can identify and pursue those things that they value. But, Sen (1999) makes it clear that the role of individual freedom is two-fold. In addition to allowing people to help themselves to lead a better life, it also enhances their capacity to influence the world in which they live. Hence the Capability Approach also leads to better political outcomes for communities and wider society. The Capability Approach has been described as ethically individualistic, as it values the freedom of each and every individual, but not ontologically individualistic (Robeyns 2003). It sees individual freedom as a means of enriching and strengthening the wider community.

The Capability Approach stresses its main purpose to be the improvement in the lives of individual people, and stands firmly opposed to analyses of development

[3]Slightly confusingly, the term 'capability' is used in two different, but inter-related ways. A person's Capability refers to his / her overall opportunities to achieve wellbeing through different functionings. But equally Sen refers to 'capabilities' in the plural which refer to the different opportunities available (such as health care / education /employment) which collectively form a 'capability set' (Robeyns 2005). In this book the two uses will be distinguished by capitalising 'Capability' when it refers to a person's overall set of opportunities.

that see economic performance as the main goal. However, it does not take a stance that is oppositional to free markets, but it is clear that the human capacity to create wealth through labour is viewed as a means to a leading a life of value, rather than an end in itself (Dreze and Sen 1995). Money is viewed as a tool that can enhance opportunities for valuable functionings, and conversely, poverty is viewed as capability destruction. Moreover, Sen recognises that there are multiple ways of leading good lives that contribute to society, that are not primarily economic activities. When applied to education, therefore the Capability Approach would recognise the value of education in preparing children and young people for future employment, but would not see this as the sum total of its purpose. It sees education as having both intrinsic and instrumental purposes (Hart 2012).

Sen saw the role of education as having two functions: to develop functioning (through what children learn at school) and to expand opportunities (thereby widening the capability set) (Saito 2003). However, he also was very clear that the purpose of education was not to build human capital, in the sense of people being seen as economic units, but was to build Capability (Saiti ibid). Sen himself was not an educationalist, and, it has been argued that he took a fairly simplistic view of education as a universal good, whereas Unterhalter (2007) has pointed out some damaging practices that go on in the name of schooling. There is a considerable body of literature that examines what form education for Capability would take. This is a discussion to which I will return.

3.6 Summary

'Wellbeing' and 'social justice' are often discursively connected, particularly in the context of schooling. I have discussed what is understood by social justice and equity in schools, by asking how we understand equality in the context of schooling. To examine this question, it was necessary to consider the purpose of schooling.

Different understandings of schooling arise from different ideological positions, particularly welfare-liberal and neo-liberal stances. The former values the intrinsic value of education and would see social justice as enhancing opportunities to lead a meaningful life. The latter values education for its economic purposes and would see social justice as enhancing the skills, knowledge and personal attributes that can be traded on the job market (human capital). This chapter has shown how both of these ideologies are at play in education, simultaneously, and explored the composite purposes of education, coupled with the implications for social justice.

Amartya Sen's Capability Approach was used to introduce the notion of social justice as the freedom to lead a life you have reason to value. In this view, the value of education in supporting individuals to become economically active is not forgotten, but this is seen to be a means to an end. Ultimately in this view, education serves to enhance opportunities to recognise and pursue those things that are value to the individual. This has considerable implications for the learning and wellbeing of children.

Chapter 4
Conceptualising Wellbeing

This chapter begins by discussing the lack of clarity around the word wellbeing before introducing five overlapping discourses of wellbeing which can be seem to be predominant in school-based policies and activities. The discussion will trace the sources of the different discourses and will demonstrate how they are used in education. This chapter serves a useful purpose in its own right, as it disentangles the 'milling mass' of different discourses that interweave in wellbeing policy. It also acts as a precursor to the critical discussion that develops later, where the different discourses of wellbeing are explored in the context of learning and other purposes of schooling.

4.1 Wellbeing – An Ill-Defined Term

Wellbeing and health are two closely related terms; indeed, they often operate together as 'health and wellbeing' and may be used interchangeably. It is a useful

J. Spratt, *Wellbeing, Equity and Education*, Inclusive Learning and Educational Equity 1, DOI 10.1007/978-3-319-50066-9_4

starting point to see how these concepts are connected. In its constitution the World Health Organisation (1948 p. 2) offered the following definition of health:

> *Health is a state of complete physical, mental and social wellbeing and not merely the absence of disease or infirmity*

The appeal of this definition lies in its emphasis on health as a positive, state of being, rather than simply absence of illness. At the time of its inception this shift from a focus on ill health to a positive notion of wellbeing was ground-breaking. Additionally, the inclusion of mental and social considerations alongside traditional medical understandings of physical health was novel. More recently there has been some criticism of this definition as being idealistic, mainly due to the inclusion of the word 'complete' (Huber, Knottnerus et al. 2011; Blair et al. 2003) as most people fall short of such a state of perfection, for much of the time. Nonetheless the World Health Organisation definition continues to be widely cited as the authoritative definition of health.

In short, then, the World Health Organisation has positioned health as a state of wellbeing. However, this does raise the question: what is meant by wellbeing? In spite of a plethora of international comparisons (UNICEF Office of Research 2013), and national frameworks (Federal Interagency Forum on Child and Family Statistics 2016, e.g. Australian Institute of Health and Welfare 2011; Office for National Statistics 2014) identifying indicators by which wellbeing can be judged, definitions of wellbeing are illusive. Notably, the national and international frameworks can only include what it is possible to know through existing statistics, and therefore they may vary from context to context and may exclude some of the more qualitative aspects of a good life.

In spite of definitional problems, the concept of wellbeing has, over recent years become ubiquitous in educational parlance (Watson et al. 2012). It is invoked in a wide range of contexts including school ethos (Spratt et al. 2006), emotional literacy (Weare 2004), resilience (Hall et al. 2009), behaviour management (Hallam 2009), school meals (Gustafsson 2004) diet and obesity (Evans and Davies 2012) and flourishing (Walker 2005). As Coleman (2009) pointed out, in the introduction to a special issue of the *Oxford Review of Education* devoted to the topic of wellbeing, there does not appear to be a consensus. Instead, he concluded that the term wellbeing is used and understood in different ways in different contexts.

Not only is wellbeing differently understood, it is linked to different agendas, as shown by Weare (2010) who described how interest groups may focus on particular aspects of mental and social wellbeing. For example, government and commercial interests may be served by skills related to employability such as relationship forming, or motivation, whilst those involved in education may see value in thinking skills, planning or resilience. Indeed, the popularity of the term may be partly explained by the broad range of positive connotations with which it is imbued (Amerijckx and Humblet 2014). However, this conflation of different concepts under one umbrella term has drawn criticism from Ecclestone and Hayes (2009b) who suggested that the contemporary focus on wellbeing in schools is based on 'slippery elision of constructs' (p. 16).

In a discourse analysis of the use of the term 'wellbeing' commissioned by the Department of Children, Schools and Families in England, Ereaut and Whiting (2008) pointed out that it was usually linked to other words (mainly at the end of the list) to convey a benign quality or 'good things'. The authors remarked that the meaning was ambiguous and unstable, commenting on the 'holographic quality' of wellbeing saying: 'Effectively, wellbeing acts like a cultural mirage: it looks like a solid construct, but when we approach it, it fragments and disappears' (p. 5). The malleability of meaning, they suggested, makes wellbeing a potentially useful concept around which to unite interagency policies and actions, whilst simultaneously making clarity illusive.

In linguistic terms wellbeing can be seen as an example of a 'floating signifier' or an 'empty signifier'. Saussure (cited in Chandler 2007) identified the distinction between the 'signifier' (in this case the word wellbeing) and the 'signified' (what the word refers to). For some words (e.g. pencil) the speaker can be reasonably confident that there is a clearly understood link between the word they use (signifier) and the actual thing to which they refer (signified). Floating signifiers may have no definite signified, but are interpreted by their linkage to other signifiers such as social justice, mental health etc. Wellbeing, to some extent derives its meaning according to what it is being discursively associated with. The conceptualisation of wellbeing is further complicated by being allied with many other floating signifiers, which themselves are open to interpretation (such as resilience, citizenship, ethos etc.). The value of linking wellbeing to these different concepts is the unquestioned air of 'good' that it brings to the topic.

Finally, it is notable that in grammatical terms wellbeing has been 'nominalised' (Fairclough 2003). This refers to the use of a noun to convey a process, for example the noun 'globalisation' refers to an ongoing process of international business and other types of exchange. The effect of such a linguistic shift can be to render opaque the decisions and actions driving a messy and complex activity to make it appear to be a tangible 'thing'. In our case we can see the adoption of the noun 'wellbeing' in preference to the verb 'being well'. Arguably, the effect of such a transformation is to remove the focus from the active part of being a well person (Watson et al. 2012). As a noun, wellbeing becomes something that can be 'done to' children, something that can be 'improved', or 'boosted', measured and recorded, rendering it ripe for policy intervention.

4.2 Identifying Discourses of Wellbeing Used in Education

As intimated in the previous section, the notion of wellbeing seems to be relevant to a range of different academic and professional disciplines, each bringing their own perspectives and assumptions. One of the aims of this book is to identify and discuss the way in which wellbeing is invoked in each of these discourses, so we can begin to unpick the complex web of discourses that swirl around in our understanding of children's wellbeing and to see the overlaps between them.

As we can see by looking at publications about indicators of wellbeing, not all the aspects of wellbeing are relevant to, or the focus of school based policies. For example, issues of parents' health, or of economic wellbeing may very well impact upon children's lives, but they are beyond the influence of the school and therefore are not part of the policy discourses of wellbeing in school. The discourses that have been identified have been selected as having relevance to the core activities of schools, and being present in policy and practice.

In seeking to identify the discourses of wellbeing in schools my work was influenced by Ereaut and Whiting's (2008) study which identified five overlapping discourses of wellbeing used in the UK government policies. In the light of my own reading of policy and analysis of data, I developed a modified version of Ereaut and Whiting's typology, still a five-fold framework, but in this model each discourse emerges from a specific academic or professional tradition. Each discourse also can trace its origins to a different period of history, ranging from the philosophy of ancient Greece, to the very contemporary concerns of sustainability.

One of the ways in which the typology used here differs from Ereaut and Whiting is that it omits their notion of 'operationalised discourse' as a discrete category. This refers to an understanding of wellbeing in which it is seen as a set of skills or actions that children should take. These, it is thought, can be directly taught and/or measured. Whilst I do not include this as a stand-alone category, the idea of operationalised understanding of wellbeing has some relevance to discourse of physical health, discourses of mental and social literacy and, in some contexts, to the discourse of care. Therefore, the concept remains important, even though it is not retained as a separate theme.

I also use a slightly different terminology, referring to the five overlapping representations (Scottish Executive 2004) of wellbeing as discursive themes. The five overlapping discursive themes of wellbeing that I work with in this book are:

Theme 1: Discourse of physical health promotion

This focuses on physical health, and health related behaviours, often discussed within the context of choice. This includes, but is not restricted to operational lists.

Theme 2: Psychological discourse of social and emotional literacy

This theme refers to discourses that may be characterised as social and emotional wellbeing and focuses on understanding and management of emotions and management of self in social situations. Similarly, this may include operational lists.

Theme 3: Discourse of care

This discursive theme links education with the field of social care of children and is most apparent in (although not exclusive to) interagency contexts. This theme is associated with ways of working and with the provision made for children by professionals. School-based concerns would include ethos, relationships and rights, often based on the concept of development of the whole child. It resonates with Ereaut and Whiting's discourse of holism.

Theme 4: Philosophical discourse of flourishing

This discursive theme derives from the Aristotelian notion of eudaimonic happiness. Influenced by more contemporary philosophy of the Capability Approach (Sen 2009) this is conceptualised by as leading a life one has reason to value.

Theme 5: Emergent discourse of sustainability

The linking of environmental sustainability with human wellbeing, mediated by a discourse of social justice is, a newly emerging discourse, and can be seen, for example, in the Marmot Report (Marmot 2010).

Regardless of how such a typology is constructed, it must be acknowledged that these discursive themes are not discrete. The following discussion of the themes will demonstrate a considerable degree of overlap, Whilst Ereaut and Whiting (2008) portray their five discursive themes as a Venn diagram with a very considerable overlap, this project is aiming to go beyond simply pointing out that commonality exists, to identify more specifically *how* these five discursive themes interact. Each of the five discourses is considered in more detail below.

4.3 Discursive Theme 1: Physical Health Promotion

As this book is focusing on the links between wellbeing and education I will begin this section by briefly looking back at how physical health has been addressed through schooling over time. Universal education, introduced in the UK at the end of the nineteenth century provided the state with its first opportunity to mediate in the lives of all its children. Until this point children had been scattered between home, work, or if they were lucky, some form of independent schooling, and no knowledge existed about the generality of children. Schooling provided a vehicle for inspection of children and they were weighed, measured and monitored, giving rise to a plethora of statistics, from which, for the first time the idea of the 'normal' child emerged.

Compulsory schooling brought to light the poor physical health of some children (Cunningham 2006) and this resulted in the foundation of a School Medical Service in 1907, with powers to undertake physical inspections (Harris 1995). Taken together with the introduction of the school meals service in 1906, this is one of the first examples of welfare-liberal reforms and is thought to be a major step towards the development of the welfare state (Harris *ibid*). Initially children's health and education were both the responsibility of local authorities and the school was the main site for addressing health. Interestingly, this also marked the beginning a shift in approaches to public health. Prior to this, the only statistics held about individual health were the causes of death. From this point onwards data was collated on the health of the living (Harris ibid).

However, with the establishment of the National Health Service (NHS) in 1948 children's health was relocated to a new government department and the role of the school diminished to being simply a site for health surveillance and mass interventions such as vaccination programmes (Blair et al. 2003; Harris 1995). The school was no longer a partner in the process. Health and education were seen as entirely separate, being the responsibility of different agencies of the state, forming a Cartesian divide between mind and body (Mayall 2001). Writing at the end of the twentieth century Mayall (1996) argued that the separation of health provision from educational provision led schools to value cognitive achievement above welfare. The division of adult labour between different government departments, she suggested had implications for professional territory which was reflected in the experiences of children in school. Although schools taught children about health, Mayall (*ibid*) observed little opportunity for children to care for their own health in the school environment, witnessing instead: lunches of poor nutritional quality, limited opportunities for exercise, and the subjugation of physical needs (such as hunger, thirst and toilet use) to the demands of the school timetable.

Somewhat ironically, a decade or so after the policy separation between providers of child health and education, an interest in children's public health was rekindled, in the context of the 'New Public Health' movement (as it was then called), which was seen as a significant paradigm shift (Ashton and Seymour 1988). The emphasis was now placed on health promotion, rather than simply detection and correction of problems. This approach demanded more 'upstream' support of health, coupled with the extension of responsibilities to professionals outside the health sector (such as teachers) as stated in the following excerpt from the Ottawa Charter for Health Promotion (World Health Organisation 1986 p. 1):

> *Health promotion is the process of enabling people to increase control over, and to improve, their health. ...... Health is a positive concept emphasizing social and personal resources, as well as physical capacities. Therefore, health promotion is not just the responsibility of the health sector, but goes beyond healthy life-styles to well-being.*

The change in focus was a move away from identification and cure of illness, to the 'empowerment' of individuals to make informed choices about the protection and promotion of their own health. A new era of partnership between health and education was ushered in. This time the focus was on fostering individual responsibility.

Much of the critique of the 'New Public Health' focused on the framing of health behaviours as individual choice, informed by education and advice to 'empower' individuals to manage their own lives, badged as 'health promotion'. Government endorsed health messages about diet, smoking, alcohol and drugs, seeking to guide healthy choices are now commonplace in developed countries. This has drawn criticism simultaneously from the political right who object to the 'nanny state' infringing the freedom of citizens to behave as they wish, and from the political left, who object to the framing of health as an individual responsibility instead of focusing on structural health inequalities (Lupton 1995).

This individualisation of the health issue, coupled with 'guidance' valorising certain behaviours is what Ereaut and Whiting (2008) refer to as an 'operationalised' approach to wellbeing. Similarly, Watson et al. (2012) refer to this approach of focusing health discussions on the actions of individuals as 'responsibilisation'. Arguably the health promotion approach is an example of 'governmentality' (Foucault 1991) or the 'conduct of conduct', brought about through state mechanisms of 'steering at a distance'. This is seen as an example of 'bio-power' whereby the government's macro level policies to produce healthy, economically active citizens are enacted at the micro level, through the dispensing of lifestyle advice by caring professionals (Gastaldo 1997). Whilst the information is conveyed in the context of personal choice the options are not neutral and some choices are clearly 'better' than others. It is argued that the state is manipulating citizens towards particular behaviours whilst simultaneously framing health as individual responsibility (Peterson and Lupton 1996). In this view, a proposal was published in the British Medical Journal, to replace the existing World Health Organisation definition of health with new twenty-first century formulation of health as 'the ability to adapt and to self-manage' (Huber et al. 2011 p. 3).

A contemporary physical health issue which schools are called on to address is the so called 'obesity epidemic'. Burrows and Wright (2007) report the introduction of self-monitoring of diet and exercise to the formal curriculum in New Zealand. In what they call 'pedagogies of surveillance' (p. 89) students are required to record and monitor their personal behaviours against an ideal. This is presented in a context of health as personal responsibility in a society infused with risk. Therefore, they argue that the opportunity to lead a life in which exercise and eating are everyday pleasures has given way to individual monitoring and training of bodies. Similarly, in the UK, Evans and Davies (2012) report that health, in policy terms has been reduced to a measurable and manageable commodity articulated as diet and exercise, with an emphasis on reaching the the 'ideal weight'. In Scotland, (a country with a reputation as a particularly unhealthy nation), a study reported that secondary school pupils viewed health in terms of individual responsibility and all participants reported self-generated regulation of food intake, sometimes coupled with feelings of guilt (Johnson et al. 2013). These discourses of 'healthism', place the responsibility for poor health on the individual and ignore the structural issues such as inequality that place some children and young people at much greater risk of unhealthy lives (Wilkinson and Pickett 2010). Thus, as Mayall (1998) commented, the discourse of choice can depoliticise childhood.

Similarly, commentators have demonstrated how sex and relationship education in schools has tended to focus on the individual management of risk rather than focusing on the positive aspects of sexual relationships (Alldred and David 2007). Blake (2008) argues that sex education in the UK is largely driven by visible, quantifiable public health outcomes, such as levels of teenage pregnancy and prevalence of sexually transmitted diseases. Whilst this is important, Blake argues there is a gap in sex education (or as he calls it, a 'hole in the bucket'), as issues of sexual pleasure are generally avoided, leaving young people unprepared for their early relationships. More recently, it has been argued that sex and relationships education has begun to overlap with education on emotional wellbeing and personal development (Moore 2012). However, this is described as calling for self-regulation as it promotes a certain emotional disposition that weighs up risks and directs the self towards correct choices (articulated as positive choices) and away from wrong (or negative choices). There is a clear overlap here with the discourses of social and emotional literacy that will be discussed in the following section. However, like the obesity agenda, contemporary sex and relationships education is criticised for focusing on individual responsibility while ignoring the socio-economic reality that the majority of teenage pregnancies occur in young women living in poverty with little opportunity to escape (Moore ibid).

It is clear, then that the Health Promotion approach has drawn considerable criticism for its focus on individual choice. However, if we revisit the original vision of public health outlined in the Ottawa Charter (World Health Organisation 1986), it is evident that it actually advocated a wider approach than simply individual responsibility. Returning to the European Network of Health Promoting Schools, we see in the 'settings approach' a vision that locates personal choice within a health promoting environment:

> *The Health Promoting School aims at achieving healthy lifestyles for the whole school population by developing supportive environments conducive to the promotion of health. It offers opportunities for and requires commitment to the provision of a social and physical environment that is safe and enhances health. A Health Promoting School uses its management structures, its internal and external relationships, its teaching and learning styles and its methods of establishing synergy with its social environment to create the means for pupils, teachers and all those involved in everyday school life to take control over and improve their physical and emotional health* (Stewart Burgher et al. 1999 p. 4)

The vision that we see portrayed here encourages personal choice within a school which provides opportunities for healthy lifestyles. Models of health promotion that focus solely on individualised lifestyle choices focus on only one aspect of this. In the above paragraph we do not see a model which shifts responsibility from state to child instead we see a school which provides a rich set of opportunities to learn about and enact good health. Thus physical health promotion discourses of choice are located within a wider supportive model which links to another discursive theme of this study – discourses of care. This provides a rich context in which to interrogate the discourses of physical health promotion in this study, exploring the extent to which they are based on individual responsibility and the extent to which they focus on the structural aspects of school provision.

4.4 Discursive Theme 2: Psychological Discourses of Social and Emotional Literacy

Humphrey, (2013) describes social and emotional learning as 'a global phenomenon that has captured the imagination of academics, policy makers and practitioners alike, in recent years' (p. 145). In *Social and emotional learning: a critical appraisal* he describes six case studies of social and emotional learning programmes in USA, England, Northern Ireland, Australia, Sweden and Singapore. The Botin Foundation, in Spain, has published a series of reports which, in total have analysed social and emotional education in 21 countries, the most recent report focusing on Denmark, Malta, Mexico, New Zealand and Switzerland (Fundacion Botin 2015). This clearly is a movement which has travelled across the globe in the last two decades.

Policy interest in the emotional lives of children has blossomed since Goleman's (1996) publication in which he famously claimed 'emotional intelligence' to be more important than Intelligence Quotient (IQ) in determining success. Leaving aside the debate about the validity of IQ as a measure of human worth (Gould 1996), it is not difficult to see why the claims made of emotional intelligence, for example, 'self-control; zeal and persistence; and the ability to motivate oneself' (Goleman 1996 p. xii), would appeal to educators. Evidence for emotional intelligence was deemed to be 'scientific', drawing from the field of brain neuroscience. Goleman's (ibid) work served to operationalise a model of emotional and social awareness and self-management, under five broad categories of: emotional self-awareness; managing emotions; harnessing emotions productively; reading emotions; and handling relationships. The first three categories relate to understanding and controlling one's internal state and the last two refer to managing oneself in social situations. All of these were promoted as skills of 'self' that could be useful in 'getting on' in life. Goleman (ibid) specifically discussed the advantages of teaching emotional literacy in schools, citing an example of 'self-science' as part of the curriculum for a class of fifth grade pupils in the United States.

The notion of emotional literacy has been widely criticised. In an extensive review of the psychological studies that would constitute an evidence base Matthews et al. (2004) suggested that the concept was so wide ranging as to be inconclusive, and that it consisted of many variables which did not correlate. Overall, they found the claims made by Goleman to be largely unsubstantiated by empirical studies. However, as Matthews et al. (ibid) pointed out, regardless of their theoretical basis Goleman's ideas became highly influential because they were successfully popularised. In this book about discourse, the debates over the robustness of the evidence base are not the key issue; what is important is the extent to which the ideas have been naturalised in contemporary educational policy and debate.

Humphrey (2013) suggests that contemporary approaches to social and emotional learning can be classified into different types. A distinction can be made between those which rely on changes to the school ethos and environment, those which involve direct curricular instruction, those which involve parents and the wider community and those which are a mixture of these approaches. A further division can be made between universal approaches that are applied to all children and targeted approaches that are used with children who are deemed to have particular social and emotional issues. What they all have in common is an assumption that children's emotions are a matter for policy intervention and few questions are asked about the legitimacy of the role of the state in the emotional lives of children.

School-based programmes to support psychological wellbeing have proliferated since the emergence of emotional intelligence as a concept, under the banner of 'emotional literacy' and later 'social and emotional learning'. The work of Weare was influential in developing practical approaches for schools, based on Goleman's ideas. At the start of the twenty-first century Weare (2000) advocated a whole school approach including consideration of relationships, anti-bullying strategies, teaching approaches and many other indirect ways of modelling and promoting good mental health and wellbeing, but soon she began to see such approaches alone as insufficient. Skills and competences, she argued should be specifically taught as part of the curriculum, declaring: 'Mental health is not caught by osmosis. More effective programmes include explicit work on the development of the relevant mental health skills in students and in staff' (Weare 2010 p. 12).

In *Developing the emotionally literate school* Weare (2004) drew from Goleman to convey emotional literacy as a set of competencies defined in three themes as: self–understanding; understanding and managing emotions and; understanding social situations and making relationships. The competencies of 'self-understanding' included having an accurate and positive self-view and possessing a sense of optimism. For the theme 'understanding and managing emotions' the competencies comprised: experiencing the whole range of emotions; understanding the causes of emotions; expressing emotions appropriately; managing emotional responses appropriately; knowing how to feel good more frequently and for longer; using information about emotions to plan and solve problems; and resilience. To 'understand social situations and make relationships' the required competencies: were forming attachments; experiencing empathy; communicating and responding to others; managing relationships; and autonomy and self-reliance. The overall focus of this approach is learning to manage the internal self, in order to operate effectively in the social world. The terminology used in this approach has become widely naturalised in the educational world.

A key argument in the justification of this work was that children's social and emotional literacy could be seen to support other goals of the schools such as improved behaviour, attendance and learning (Weare 2004; Hallam 2009). Moreover, some writers have commented on how 'social and emotional learning' has been blurred with character education, whereby young people are encouraged to develop traits such as empathy, resilience, determination and application (Ecclestone 2012). As Arthur (2005) points out, governments tend to promote character traits that are of instrumental value to the state. These issues will be considered further in Chap. 5, where the discourses of wellbeing will be discussed in relation to learning.

The social and emotional learning approach to wellbeing has been critiqued from various angles. The question of evidence remains a key issue for social and emotional learning to this day, with Humphrey (2013) commenting 'it is perhaps fair to say that its growth in popularity has been faster than the evidence base on which it rests' (p. 145). Certainly early programmes, such as England's Social and Emotional Aspects of Learning (SEAL) programme were accused of large-scale introduction in advance of any evidence of their effects (Craig 2007) although it must be acknowledged that the evidence in this field is growing rapidly.

Programmes have also been criticised for taking an overly prescriptive, and individualised view of wellbeing. By focussing on a pre-defined operational list of attributes, determined by professional adults, it is argued that a concept of wellbeing has been developed that takes no account of the ways that children themselves experience or understand wellbeing (Coppock 2010). The imposition of a single dominant framework on the professional understanding of childhood wellbeing results in the loss of voices of minority groups, who may prioritise different issues (Watson et al. 2012). Moreover, the operationalised model is largely individualised, taking little account of the situational nature of social and emotional wellbeing. Watson et al. (2012), who conceive wellbeing to be: subjectively experienced; contextual and embedded; and relational, argue that the understanding of wellbeing as a universal set of individualised skills is an inappropriate way to conceptualise a good childhood.

A different type of critique is articulated by Ecclestone (2007) and Ecclestone and Hayes (2009a, b). These authors are deeply critical of the extent to which the state, through the medium of schooling, is currently intervening in the emotional lives of children. Drawing from Furedi (2004) they argue that current trends in education have taken a 'therapeutic turn' which assumes all children to be emotionally vulnerable, requiring the support of professionals to develop into fully functioning emotional and social beings. This is portrayed as a limited view of human potential, which has created 'the rise of the diminished self' (Ecclestone 2007), which is thought to be damaging for two main reasons. Firstly, a programme of professional intervention in the emotional lives of children conveys assumptions of universal deficit which will act as self-fulfilling prophecy, if children accept this version of themselves as weak, vulnerable and in need of external emotional support. Thus, they suggest that this approach will undermine agency and autonomy instead of promoting the resilient and self-confident individuals it seeks to foster (Ecclestone and Hayes 2009b). Secondly Ecclestone and Hayes (2009a) argue that by changing the curriculum to devote timetabled lessons to 'therapeutic' subjects, and also by adapting teaching approaches to be more personally relevant, that the subject content of the traditional academic disciplines is diluted, and that we are failing properly to educate our children. Therefore, they argue, the emphasis on emotional aspects of schooling has resulted in 'changing the subject' in two senses: enhancing the sense of vulnerability of the individual subject, and eroding the academic standing of the school subjects.

There is also a growing body of writers, (largely, though not exclusively, philosophers), who object strongly to the idea that childhood wellbeing can be divided into itemised lists of personal constructs, arguing that being a fully functioning human is a much more complex endeavour than being able to operationalise series of descriptors (e.g. Clack 2012). For example, Suissa (2008) asks, 'in what sense can forming and sustaining "productive relationships" or "caring for others" be described as "skills"?' (p. 582). Similarly, Fielding argues that contemporary approaches encourage children to 'do' relationships rather than to 'have' friends (Fielding 2011). These critiques hold that teaching social and emotional literacy is limiting in its scope, and suggest instead that emotions are better developed through life experiences and learning.

Although this section has focused on social and emotional learning, it should be noted that other approaches to 'teaching happiness' have emerged over the last decade, which include aspects of emotional literacy, but claim to take a wider perspective on life than simply emotional management. 'Positive Psychology' (Seligman et al. 2009) represents happiness in three domains, each of which, it is claimed, is measurable and skill based. The three domains are: hedonic happiness (joy, love contentment and pleasure, collectively referred to as the 'good stuff'); a state of flow (the engaged life, being totally absorbed in what is happening); and the meaningful life (increased connect to others, and knowing where your strengths lie). This appears to be something of an amalgamation of psychology and philosophy, and Seligman (2011) acknowledges influences of Aristotle on his thinking. These ideas have been adopted by Wellington College, an English public school, which teaches 'happiness' through a cyclical process of self-management characterised as 'awareness', 'intervention' and 'action', delivered through a curriculum that includes: caring for the body; philosophy and wellbeing; emotions; resilience; strength and flow; relationships (Morris 2009). We can see in this approach something of an overlap between the psychological discourse of emotional and social learning and the philosophical discourse of flourishing.

However, Suissa (2008) mounts a scathing attack on the claims of Positive Psychology to Aristotelian roots, suggesting it acknowledges his work whilst side-stepping its significance. She suggests that the field of positive psychology is an attempt to produce empirical answers to philosophical questions about happiness. This is an example of overlap between two of the discursive themes, in this case identifying some tension between them.

4.5 Discursive Theme 3: Discourse of Care

In the previous two sections (discourse of physical health promotion, and psychological discourses of social and emotional literacy) the focus has very much been on the responsibilisation of the individual child, through strategies of self-management. The discourse of care focusses not on the state of the child, but on the provisions of care made for children by adults. Contemporary discussions of wellbeing often invoke the notion of the 'whole child' in the context of his/her relationships, and call for professionals to take a 'holistic' view of their responsibilities. This is linked to the way in which children's rights are enacted, particularly the rights to participation in decisions made about themselves. In the school context it takes account of the relationships and ethos within the school and of interagency efforts to enhance childhood wellbeing.

In exploring what is meant by the education of the 'whole child', Noddings (2005b) criticises the 'legacy of bureaucratic thought' (p. 12) that, in pursuit of efficiency, portrays humans as a collection of discrete attributes and needs, which can be mapped onto different curricular areas or professional responsibilities. Instead she suggests that teachers and pupils should meet and respond to each other as whole persons, unrestrained by the fragmented nature of current school activities. Noddings (ibid) calls for all teachers to take sensitive account of moral, social, emotional and aesthetic questions within their curricular area, and points to the need for an overall climate of trust within a school, suggesting approaches such as 'gentle but persistent invitations to all students to participate', 'less competition' and 'warmer hospitality for parents'. However, she also cautions that even when consciously attempting to work with 'whole children' it is difficult to avoid the temptation to describe the whole in terms of its constituent parts, locating each aspect in a particular place in the curriculum or other organisational structure of the school.

Noddings (2005a) also raises questions about what we mean when we talk about 'caring' for children. In a caring relationship there are two parties – the carer and the cared-for. Whilst in many natural relationships the carer and cared-for may be interchangeable roles, in a professional caring relationship, these roles are generally fixed, for example the teacher is the carer and the child is cared-for. Noddings (ibid) distinguishes between two forms of meaning attached to the concept of caring in a professional context. In one interpretation, care is a virtue of the carer, who makes decisions on behalf of the cared-for, believing them to be in the best interests of the cared-for. In some cases, caring is seen as a 'pedagogical virtue' demonstrated by insisting that students acquire the knowledge and skills that have been prescribed. In this situation, the cared-for may have no awareness of a caring aspect to the relationship, and might even believe the opposite to be the case. For Noddings (ibid), whatever claims the professional might make, if the cared-for does not feel cared for, then this is not a caring relationship, but more likely a controlling relationship.

This understanding of 'care' as something which is 'done to' children is predicated on developmental understandings of childhood in which children are seen as passive 'empty vessels' in need of socialisation by adults. According to Hendrick (2005) this understanding of childhood has underpinned most large scale professional interventions since the start of compulsory schooling. Hendrick (1997) suggests that state intervention in childhood serves to normalise children. Arguing that children are seen as investments for the future of the nation, he suggests that the school is responsible for socialising children in ways which will be seen as beneficial to society. Thus, he suggests, the extensive network of professionals working with children, whilst ostensibly caring, in fact has a coercive role (Hendrick 2003). Likewise, feminist writers have highlighted how caring relationships are imbued with power relationships, that actions undertaken by professionals in the name of 'care' may not always be truly caring and may even, in some cases, be damaging (Cockburn 2011).

In order for the relationship to be properly called caring, Noddings (2005b) contends that it must be an encounter to which both parties contribute. Central to the truly caring relationship is dialogue, as it through open ended conversations that a common search for understanding, empathy and appreciation can take place. Hence, the teacher is interested not only in the needs of the child as assumed by the school, or the current policy, but is attendant to the expressed needs of children (Noddings 2012). Dialogue also allows the carer to evaluate the effects of the attempts to care. An ethic of care is based on complex, multi-directional relationships where decision making draws on ethical concerns interpreted in particular circumstances, and as such cannot be contained by rules and predetermined boundaries (Watson et al. 2012).

Not only is care conceived to be at the root of teacher-pupil relationships, but Fielding (2011), offers a vision of a school community based on caring relationships between all:

> *Community is a process in which human beings regard each other in a certain way (love, care and concern for the other) and in which they relate to each other and act together in mutuality as persons, not as role occupants. It is, furthermore, a mutuality informed by the values of freedom (freedom to be and become yourself) and equality (equal worth), which condition each other reciprocally and preserve the integrity of individuality through the heterocentric insistence on their care and delight for each other (p 51).*

This conception of a trusting, caring relationship between children and teachers based on a search for mutual respect and understanding resonates with contemporary ideas of children as active participants in shaping their own lives. Developments in the sociology of childhood, at the end of the twentieth century challenged the understanding of childhood as a stage of passive development (Prout and James 1997; Mayall 2000, 2002). The recognition of childhood agency has had far reaching implications for the ways in which professionals structure their work with children (Prout 1999).

The new ideas in the sociology of childhood heralded an emphasis on the rights of children, and had a particular resonance with the participation rights accorded to children by the United Nations Convention on the Rights of the Child (United Nations 1989). Article 12.1 accorded children and young people the right to 'express views freely in all matters affecting the child', and for those views to be given 'due weight in accordance with the age and maturity of the child,' This reframed the child as a competent being with a right to control aspects of his or her life. The research and policy response to this was a proliferation of ideas about how children could be involved in decisions about themselves and a focus on children's voices, coupled with fierce critiques of how such interventions were implemented (Hill, Davis et al. 2004; Morrow 2006; Vandenroeck and Bouverne-De Bie 2006).

Wyness (2001) identified an inherent conflict between children's rights to welfare and their rights to self-determination. On one hand, welfare rights place a responsibility on adults in authority to provide what they perceive children need, and thus, he argues, strengthen the hold that adults have over children. On the other hand, rights to self-determination require adults to respond to demands children make to be heard. However, respecting the views of children and paying attention to their welfare need not necessarily be viewed as antagonistic.

Brighouse (2002) suggests that children are not always best placed to make choices that would be to their benefit in the longer term, since due to inexperience they may not be fully able to understand the implications of some of their actions. Thus, adults have a role in protecting children's present and future interests. At the same time, he argues, this does not negate the importance of taking account of children's views and fostering the development of agency. Thus, rather than envisaging a conflict between the control of children for the benefit of their welfare and their freedom for self-determination, he sees care of children as a balance between the two, with a shift with age towards the freedom of the child. This is entirely congruent with Noddings' (2005b) understanding of true care where, through the dialogic relationship the child understands that he/she is cared for and that where adults seek to direct children this is accompanied with discussions, explanations and negotiations. Hence, it is argued that education that is underpinned by an ethic of care creates a space for eudaimonic approaches to wellbeing (Watson et al. 2012).

This section has explored issues that can be seen to be pertinent to discourses of care of children, and, in particular has demonstrated that care of children may be interpreted in different ways by professionals. Whilst the focus in this section has been on two types of care identified by Noddings, a third type of care has been described by Fielding (2007), who refers to 'simulacra of care'. This is pretence at the 'true' form of dialogic caring, with the purpose of manipulating children into meeting goals set by others. Fielding's paper is discussed in some depth in Chap. 5.

4.6 Discursive Theme 4: Philosophical Discourse of Flourishing

This section will demonstrate how contemporary philosophical discussions of wellbeing draw from the work of Aristotle and his understanding of happiness. Therefore, the discussion of flourishing, as we understand it today is preceded by a short section outlining the ideas of the ancient philosopher.

4.6.1 Aristotle's Notion of Happiness

When philosophers talk of wellbeing they often draw from Aristotle's concept of happiness, which is generally represented in contemporary language with the word 'flourishing'. To understand this concept, we should first consider different understandings of the word 'happiness' – a topic which has been debated for millennia.

A distinction can be made between hedonic and eudaimonic happiness. Hedonia has been defined as 'the presence of positive affect and the absence of negative affect' (Deci and Ryan 2008). It is a subjective state of pleasure, applying to the present moment, which may be transient. By contrast Aristotle's (1985) (translated Irwin) notion of eudaimonia is a longer term sense of fulfilment derived from leading a 'good' life. For him, happiness was not simply the enjoyment of short term amusements, or an emotional response to the ups and downs of daily life, but it was a state of 'flourishing' involving self-actualisation, and a sense of self-determination, expressed by Deci and Ryan (2008) as being 'fully functioning'. Hedonic happiness has an inward looking focus on feelings and emotions, whereas eudaimonia has an outward looking focus on how a life is lived in relation to the wider world.

Clearly, there is some relationship between hedonia and eudaimonia as long-term fulfilment may well impact positively on short-term feelings of pleasure. Equally, feelings of happiness in the present may be more motivating towards the sorts of behaviours that may be necessary for longer term, fulfilment. However, over-ardent pursuit of short term happiness (hedonism) may cause longer term damage to wellbeing, for example through involvement with alcohol or drugs. John Stewart Mill's (1861) work on Utilitarianism is associated with a hedonic understanding of happiness, suggesting that 'pleasure and freedom from pain are the only things desirable as ends' (p. 275). However, Mill held that some sources of pleasure (notably pleasures of the mind) were preferable to the pleasures 'of which swine are capable' (p. 258), so his notion of happiness was not entirely divorced from Aristotle's.

Gasper (2004) suggested that a hedonic view of happiness, by reducing wellbeing to 'well-feeling', frames people as simple, malleable creatures, with limited intrinsic resource and a unidimensional system of pleasure. By contrast, he suggested the Aristotelian tradition of eudaimonic happiness assumes people are multi-faceted, reasoning, social and moral actors. In this view wellbeing is seen as the fulfilment of the complex nature which is intrinsic to each individual, which Gasper characterises as 'well-living'. Whilst a hedonic stance sees wellbeing as individualised and personal, a eudaimonic stance sees wellbeing as both a private and a public good, since for many people a well lived life entails positive contributions to the lives of others (Keyes 2006). Hence, Deci and Ryan (2008) suggest that hedonic and eudaimonic analyses of happiness are based on different understandings of what it means to be human. Perhaps, therefore it is not surprising that these two understandings of wellbeing are located in different academic disciplines, with psychology leaning towards hedonic understandings and philosophy favouring eudaimonic analyses (Keyes 2006).

In terms of this book, which is looking at the discourses of wellbeing that are most important in education, hedonia is not a key topic. Whilst schools are attendant to the emotions of children, these are most apparent through the foci on social and emotional literacy. In some senses it might be argued that schools are anti-hedonia as they encourage children, during working hours, to put aside their games and devote their time to learning activities that may serve longer term purposes. Conversely, eudaimonia is a central theme to education, as will be discussed below, as education surely has the potential to create opportunities for flourishing in the present and in the future (even if does not always do so).

For Aristotle (1985) happiness was the ultimate 'good' in life and was not the means to achieve other ends. Eudaimonic happiness was achieved through the way a person lived, and Aristotle attached importance to the autonomous decisions that allowed individuals to decide what for them was 'the good'. Living a 'noble' or 'virtuous' life was thought to be essential to happiness. Virtue was achieved, in part, through interactions with other people, so whilst eudaimonia was based on individual freedom to choose, it was not simply about an individual's feelings, it was interlinked with the good he did in the world.

In some ways Aristotle's philosophy does not translate easily into contemporary society, as it can be interpreted as exclusive (Biesta 2010). Firstly, in ancient Athens only free men (not women, children or slaves) were thought to be able to develop the necessary powers of reasoning to be able to decide how to lead a virtuous life. Secondly, for Aristotle (1985) the purest form of happiness was achieved through contemplative philosophical thought. In the twenty-first century most people would consider a much wider range of activities to be meaningful, and we would not suggest that only those engaged in deeply theoretical activities could flourish. In spite of this dissonance between the ancient and modern worlds Aristotle's basic premise of happiness as flourishing through leading a meaningful life remains influential in philosophical and political thinking today, albeit with a wider interpretation of who or what might be included in the analysis. We now move to consider how these ideas are used in contemporary contexts.

4.6.2 Contemporary Understandings of Flourishing

A philosopher, writing about the wellbeing of children in the school context, White (2011), uses twenty-first century vocabulary to articulate a similar vision of wellbeing as 'fulfilment' which is conceptualised as 'wholehearted engagement' in 'worthwhile activities and relationships', which are, in the main successful. Again we see wellbeing as an active ongoing dynamic process associated with the way in which an individual life is led, and we see not only an emphasis on personal doings, but also relationships. Pursuits which contribute to a person's own good, he suggests, often have others at their heart. Whereas Aristotle cautioned against confusing 'amusement' with happiness, White offers a modern equivalent where wellbeing should not be conflated with desire fulfilment through consumerism. This raises questions about what is worthwhile and who decides. Using extreme examples of 'sand-counters' or those who perpetually lie in bed, White suggests that while we cannot prescribe what is or is not worthwhile to others it should be 'personally significant' and 'based on relevant information'.

Amartya Sen developed the Capability Approach based on a eudaimonic understanding of wellbeing. The Capability Approach sees wellbeing as an issue of social justice, suggesting that opportunities for wellbeing of citizens, rather than economic prosperity should form the basis of governmental analyses of progress (Sen 2009). He argues that wellbeing is about how you lead your life, or your possible range of 'beings and doings' or 'functionings' (Sen 1992). Wellbeing is conceptualised in the Capability Approach as leading 'the kind of lives we have reason to value' (Sen 1999 p. 14); a definition which leaves the determination of what is valuable to the individual. However, by using the expression has '*reason* to value', he suggests wellbeing requires that individuals consciously weigh up the values of different activities.

Achievement of wellbeing is supported or restricted by the opportunities an individual has to develop their 'functionings' or their 'beings and doings'. The term 'Capability' refers to the freedom a person has to achieve wellbeing (or lead a life s/he has reason to value). Capability, then,is not only concerned with outcomes; it is concerned with opportunities available to individuals to achieve wellbeing (Sen 2009). The expansion of a person's capabilities or opportunities to choose, what for them is a life of value is seen in the Capability Approach as the appropriate variable by which to judge equality.

Linked to the concept of Capability as freedom to achieve wellbeing, Sen (1999) identifies some basic capabilities which are prerequisites to wellbeing. These include health, education, political freedom, economic facilities and protective security. Significantly, the Capability Approach rejects analyses which view wellbeing as directly related to wealth or income, but does acknowledge that money is an 'admirable general-purpose means to have more freedom to lead the kind of lives we have reason to value' (Sen 1999 p. 14). Barriers to wellbeing or 'unfreedoms' are identified as such things as undernutrition, inadequate health care, lack of access to education, denial of civic rights etc., many, but not all of which link to economic hardship. Poverty is seen as 'capability deprivation' as it denies opportunities to lead a life of value.

Nussbaum (2011) frames human Capability in terms of a life worthy of human dignity. She proposes ten 'central capabilities', which she suggests should be provided to all citizens of a 'decent political order'. Briefly, these are: life (not dying prematurely); bodily health; bodily integrity; senses, imagination and thought; emotions; practical reason; affiliation (living with others); concern for other species; play; and control over one's environment (political and material). Some of these capabilities are particularly relevant to this book, as they make a direct link between education and wellbeing, offering a view of the type of education which might foster capabilities. For example, the basic capability 'senses, imagination and thought' is exemplified as:

> *Being able to use the senses, to imagine, think and reason – and to do these things in a "truly human" way, a way informed and cultivated by an adequate education, including, but by no means limited to, literacy and basic mathematical and scientific training.* (Nussbaum 2011 p. 41)

Thus, in this view wellbeing encompasses what Nussbaum calls 'freedom of the mind' (Nussbaum 2006). This will be discussed further in the following chapter which explores the discursive relationships between learning and wellbeing.

Although the Capability Approach centres on the freedom of individuals to achieve wellbeing, it draws from a eudaimonic view of flourishing which is described by Giovanola (2005) as 'anthropological richness'. Rather than proposing a form of 'radical individualism', he suggests that flourishing can be seen as 'realising the higher Good in a virtuous life in the highly important context of social relations and friendships' (Giovanola 2005 p. 262). It values the freedom and wellbeing of each and every individual, but sees this as a driver, not for the pursuit of self-interest, but for enriching the wider community, strengthening social life rather than fragmenting it (Walker 2005).

Within the Capability literature there is recognition that children hold a different position to that of adults. Since agency and self-determination are key to choosing a life you have reason to value the debate around children as both active agents in the present and 'adults in the making' (Mayall 1998), receives some attention. Sen, (who is not an educationalist) holds a position that for children, it is not their freedom in the present that is important, but rather it is the freedom they will have in the future that should be considered by their parents and teachers (Saito 2003). For example, we place constraints upon the autonomy of children through the requirements of schooling in order to protect or promote their capabilities (Biggeri et al. 2006). Therefore, children's functionings, their beings and doings, are often seen as a more appropriate evaluative space than capabilities. Thus, MacLeod (2010) suggests:

> *What matters for children is not the opportunity to achieve health or have emotional attachments, but being healthy and having emotional attachments (p 185).*

Moreover, Capability and wellbeing are more closely aligned for children than they are for adults, because their responsibilities are different. For adults Capability is the freedom to choose a life which a person has reason to value, and this may involve choosing to prioritise the welfare of others above one's own wellbeing. Indeed, for Sen (2009), the more highly developed a person's capabilities, the greater the responsibility to consider wider issues than their own wellbeing. However, whilst children are encouraged to think of others before themselves in matters of courtesy, charity or friendship, we do not expect children to compromise their overall wellbeing for the benefit of others. Where this does occur, such as in child labour, it is viewed as an 'unfreedom'. Nussbaum (2011) states clearly that 'Capability destruction' in children should be viewed as a grave matter and should always be viewed as 'off limits'.

However, as the study of childhood Capability has developed, a more nuanced understanding is emerging, which tries to account for the complexities of children as both 'beings and becomings' (Uprichard 2008). Children are seen as both capable and needy relying on adults to create the conditions in which their functionings and capabilities are fostered, both in the present and for the future (Nussbaum 2006). Hence children's capabilities are regarded as qualitatively different from adults and childhood is seen as a dynamic period of Capability expansion (Ballet et al. 2011). In addition to providing for the wellbeing of children in the present, the development of Capability requires that as children mature their freedom of choice is encouraged as they develop the capacity to make informed decisions and to evaluate and revise their choices (ibid). However, it is by understanding themselves as unique individuals that children will develop the capacity to choose what, for them, is a life of value. Consequently, the Capability Approach is linked to the development of 'personhood' and the notion of 'human richness' (Giovanola 2005) and wellbeing of children has been conceptualised as the 'unfolding' of each child's 'inner diversity' or 'unique potential' (Kickbusch, Gordon et al. 2012 p. 28). In this view, childhood is not simply a phase of socialising into the existing status quo, but it is a time in which, given appropriate conditions, every individual can uniquely come ‘into presence’ (Biesta 2010 p. 80). From this discussion it is evident that there is considerable resonance between the discursive theme of ‘care’ and the discursive theme of ‘flourishing’ as both ask important questions about the balance between the agency of children and the responsibility of adults.

The philosophical discourses of the Capability Approach which conceptualises childhood wellbeing in terms of ‘valuable beings and doings’, linked to the development of agency and personhood, have significant implications for education. Work in the area has developed considerably in recent years, and there is a growing literature interrogating the role of schooling in the development of Capability, which will inform some of the discussions in the next chapter.

4.7 Discursive Theme 5: The Emergent Theme of Sustainability

Whilst environmental sustainability has been a public concern for decades, connections between sustainability, equality and wellbeing have emerged more recently. When Ereaut and Whiting (2008) undertook their discourse analysis of the use of wellbeing in UK public policy, they described the policy discourse of sustainability in this context as newly emerging. There has been growing interest in sustainability in schools in the intervening years, yet I would argue that this remains an emergent, although changing, discourse of wellbeing in schools at the time of writing. This section will briefly review some of the key issues that link issues of sustainability to discourses of wellbeing.

As the impact human activity on the environment becomes increasingly evident, commentators have noted how the deleterious effects of environmental damage are more harshly experienced by poorer people. This is true on an international level, where poorer, more marginalised countries are less able to cope with environmental change, and often more exposed to climatic disasters. It is also true at an individual level, where within any country, people living in conditions of poverty are more exposed to pollution, have less access to limited natural resources and less able to respond to disasters such as floods (Adger and Winkels 2007).

A strategic review of health inequalities in England (Marmot 2010) reiterated the well-documented relationship between ill health and poverty (Acheson 1998; Townsend and Davidson 1982), but also pointed to the unequal impact that climate change could have on different groups of people. Wealthy people, the report suggested have greater opportunities to live in more favourable environmental conditions, and are better able to access scarce resources. In this vein the report states:

> *The fair distribution of health, well-being and sustainability are important social goals. Tackling social inequalities in health and tackling climate change must go together (p 15).*

The inequalities created and reproduced by exposure to environmental hazards play out differently in different contexts, for example in the United States this is an issue which is associated with racial discrimination, but it is always also linked socio-economic disadvantage, prompting Agyman (2007) to comment that

> *Sustainability is at least as much about politics, injustice and inequality as it is about science, technology or the environment. (p. 178)*

Thus we can see that human wellbeing is deeply entangled with the way in which we care for the environment. Whereas, in the past, environmental damage was justified by the arguments that the products of such activity enhanced wellbeing (by providing materials that improved people's quality of life), increasingly we can see that the balance has shifted, so we have reached a tipping point where a more polluted or depleted world will have deleterious effects on wellbeing (Dietz and Rosa 2009). The link between sustainability and human happiness was clearly expressed in the inaugural 'World Happiness Report' (Helliwell et al. 2012) Taking a eudaimonic view of happiness the report states:

> *....if we act wisely we can protect the Earth while raising quality of life broadly around the world. We can do this by adopting lifestyles and technologies that improve happiness (or life satisfaction) while reducing human damage to the environment. 'Sustainable development' is the term given to the combination of human well-being, social inclusion and environmental sustainability. We can say that the quest for happiness is intimately linked to the quest for sustainable development. P4*

Clearly, then sustainability has been established as intricately connected to wellbeing. For the purposes of this book, we now need to turn our attention to the implications of this relationship for education, to examine how this is impacting on the discursive treatment of wellbeing in schools.

A report by the Australian Research Institute in Education for Sustainability (ARIES), provided reports on sustainability education from countries including China, New Zealand, Sweden, Scotland, Ireland and South Africa as well as Australian projects (Henderson and Tilbury 2004). At this time there was an interest in education for sustainability, yet, interestingly, in this 57-page document the word wellbeing appears only twice. Little over a decade ago, in educational circles the sustainability discourse of wellbeing was not well developed.

However, since then a body of work has emerged which encourages schools to explore ways of encouraging children to develop a greater appreciation of the natural world through outdoor learning, and hands-on experience of nature. Not only is thought to foster a lifelong concern for the environment and sustainability issues (Knight 2013) many claims are made for a positive effect of interaction with nature on social and emotional wellbeing. For example, learning out of doors is thought to enhance: working with others; self-confidence; relationships with peers and relationships with staff (Maller and Townsend 2006). Young children (aged 3–4) working out of doors were reported to be calmer, more focussed and have more positive social reactions (Nedovic and Morrissey 2013). Moreover, outdoor activities are claimed to have pedagogical benefits as the unpredictability of nature provides enhanced learning opportunities, and the teacher has more of a chance to understand the 'whole child', in an environment which escapes from the rigidity of classroom norms and behaviours (Waite 2010).

Recently, Forest Schools, originating in Denmark, have grown in international popularity, albeit with slightly different enactments in different countries (Knight 2013). The UK Forest School Association which was set up in 2012 claims that 'Forest School is an inspirational process that offers all learners regular opportunities to achieve, develop confidence and self-esteem through hands-on learning experience in a local woodland or natural environment with trees' (cited in Knight 2013 p. 5). It aims to 'promote holistic development of those involved, fostering resilient, confident, independent and creative learners (cited in Knight 2013 p. 6). Whilst Forest Schools are not widely available to all children, and also focus on younger age groups, we can see, in their materials a strong link between sustainability and the lexicon of social and emotional literacy. These kinds of connections are beginning to permeate educational discourse more generally.

In conclusion, then, it appears that the sustainability discourse of wellbeing continues to develop within the educational community. It is interesting to note how this discourse overlaps with other discourses of wellbeing. In particular, the outdoor learning movement is adopting the discourses of social and emotional wellbeing that have become almost naturalised in educational policy. Yet, this is actually a marked difference from the political links made between sustainability and wellbeing in the earlier part of this section, and indeed the rationale for sustainability education itself. Writers outside of education seem more concerned with the opportunities to live well (the philosophical discourse of flourishing), whereas when this topic migrated into education, close connections with nature also became linked to emotional literacy.

4.8 Summary

The concept of wellbeing has gained a great deal of currency over the last decade and is particularly prominent in policy debates about children and young people. Yet the term is ill-defined and used in a range of different contexts. In this chapter it was shown how the term wellbeing, as used in the context of schooling, emerges from a range of professional and academic disciplines each with their own understanding of the meaning. Whilst this multi-disciplinary buy-in allows wellbeing to be the focus of inter-professional effort and discussion it can also lead to misunderstandings and confusion. Five main discursive themes of wellbeing were identified and discussed: discourse of physical health promotion, discourse of social and emotional literacy, discourse of care, philosophical discourse of flourishing and emergent discourse of sustainability.

Chapter 5
Conceptualising Relationships Between Learning and Wellbeing

5.1 Introduction

Having discussed the concept of 'wellbeing' in some detail, we now turn our attention the issue that prompted this work in the first place; the relationships between wellbeing and the main function of school, learning. What do pronouncements such as 'learning and health go hand in hand', (Scottish Health Promoting Schools Unit 2004) mean and how are they understood? Using the different discursive themes of wellbeing identified in Chap. 4, I will now examine how these are invoked in the context of learning.

Chapter 3 explored the purposes of education, and in so doing identified a range of ways in which the term 'learning' could be understood. It is clear that schooling has multiple purposes, seeking not only to guide what children know, and can

J. Spratt, *Wellbeing, Equity and Education*, Inclusive Learning and Educational Equity 1, DOI 10.1007/978-3-319-50066-9_5

do, but it also seeks to shape children's dispositions, attitudes and characters in various ways. Learning, in the contemporary context includes learning how to be a particular type of person; a position that invites state intervention in some very personal aspects of children's lives. A distinction was made between learning as socialisation, designed to shape children's development to fit in with pre-determined notions of the status quo, and learning as subjectification, aiming to support children to understand and foster their uniqueness and individuality (Biesta 2010). Similarly, a distinction was made between learning which served narrow economic purposes and broader notions of learning as an intrinsic good in which children learnt 'to be human' (Macmurray 2012).

The policy appropriation of childhood wellbeing, and its explicit link to learning, in its broadest sense, raise important questions about how these policies are shaped and enacted. Given that both 'learning' and 'wellbeing' have multiple interpretations and can be linked to different agendas, it is reasonable to ask what is going on, and whose purposes are being served when a discourse of wellbeing is invoked in the context of learning. Drawing from the work of Michael Fielding (2007) I will make a distinction between educational practices in which wellbeing serves learning and those in which the purpose of learning is to foster the wellbeing of students. The first of these models is framed in a neo-liberal ideology, in which personal aspects of wellbeing are harnessed in order to enhance the forms of learning which serve the performativity of the school. The second is framed in a welfare-liberal ideology in which the purpose of education is to expand the opportunities for human flourishing. The roles of the different discursive themes of wellbeing within these two models are discussed.

In Chap. 4, five discursive themes of wellbeing were identified (discourse of physical health promotion, discourse of social and emotional literacy, discourse of care, philosophical discourse of flourishing and the emergent discourse of sustainability). This was a largely descriptive account, linking the themes to different academic and professional disciplines. In the discussion that follows, the educational purposes of the wellbeing agenda are explored. In demonstrating how discourses of wellbeing can be utilised in different ways to support seemingly distinct political ideologies, this chapter takes a more critical stance, as issues of politics, power and control begin to enter the discussion.

5.2 Fielding's Typology of Schooling

The arguments that follow draw from a paper by Michael Fielding (2007). In *The human cost and intellectual poverty of high performance schooling: radical philosophy, John Macmurray and the remaking or person-centred education,* Fielding presented a fourfold typology of schools which explored the relationship between what he termed the functional and the personal aspects of education. In the section that follows Fielding's typology will be described in some detail before building on these ideas to apply them to the key focus for this study, i.e. the discourse of wellbeing in education.

Fielding drew from the work of the Scottish philosopher John Macmurray, who was concerned with the nature of self. Rejecting atomistic views of individuals, he saw humans as 'deeply situated communal beings whose personhood is steeped in mutuality' (Macmurray 1941 cited in Fielding 2007, p. 386). The self, in Macmurray's view entirely depended upon, and was shaped by, the relationships in which it was involved.

In particular Fielding (ibid) works with Macmurray's distinction between functional and personal relationships. Functional relationships were seen as instrumental, with a purpose defined by and limited to the activity that takes place within that relationship. For example, a bus driver transports a person from place to place, and that is the sum total of the relationship. By contrast, Macmurray conceived personal relationships as those which help us to become ourselves. The shared activities are expressive of the personal relationship, but do not define it. Thus, we might choose to go to the beach with our friends to enjoy each other's company, but the friendship is not in any way limited to beach expeditions. At the macro level, Macmurray saw functional relationships as constituting 'society' and personal relationships constituting 'community'.

The two forms of relationship were thought to depend upon each other but were not easily separable. Functional relationships, Macmurray argued were essential to support the personal aspects of life. However, he viewed the two as unequal, claiming that the functional should be subservient to the personal, saying 'the functional life is for the personal, the personal life is through the functional life' (Macmurray 1941 cited in Fielding 2007, p. 398). However, he noted, this is not always the case. Writing during World War II, Macmurray observed extremes of personal sacrifice for functional ends. He commented that although the two cannot be kept apart 'if the personal life cannot control the working life it will have to fetch and carry for it' (ibid, p. 389).

Fielding (2004, 2007) used the concepts of functional and personal, and the relations between them to develop a fourfold model of modern-day schooling.[1] He interpreted the functional aspect of schooling to be the processes which focussed on educational products such as targets and qualifications, and the personal aspect to be a meaningful personal development which was communally situated. His four models are as follows:

The impersonal organisation. The functional marginalises the personal. The focus is entirely on educational products.

The affective community. The personal marginalises the functional. An over-emphasis on the emotional compromises academic learning.

---

[1]Fielding (2012) has recently further developed this typology to include a fifth category, the 'school as agent of democratic fellowship'. In this category the *political* supports the personal. This goes beyond the scope of my focus on the relationship between learning and wellbeing and therefore will not be considered in detail here.

The high performance learning organisation. The personal is for the sake of the functional. Emotions are engaged by the organisation in order to enhance performativity.

The person centred learning community. The functional is for the sake of the personal. Learning is seen as valuable when individual personal development takes place in the context of a democratic learning community.

For the purpose of my work, which is looking at the interplay between wellbeing and learning, the first two categories which focus exclusively on either the personal or the functional in isolation are not relevant. However, Fielding's discussion of the final two categories are very illuminating. In the high performance learning organisation and the person centred learning community there is a focus on the interactions between learning (functional) and the affective aspects of schooling, that could loosely be called wellbeing (personal), which resonates with the purposes of this study. Fielding himself, also thought that that these two categories merited most attention, commenting that, superficially the two models, could be seen as similar, as both pay attention to the education and the wellbeing of their pupils, but he says, in reality:

> *They are worlds apart; their felt realties are utterly at odds with each other (p. 398)*

Both types of school could adopt the same language of care, but lying beneath that may be very different ideologies. To Fielding, it is their apparent similarity that suggests that there may be important underlying issues meriting closer scrutiny. There follows a summary of these two models of schooling.

The High Performance Learning Organisation Relationships in these schools are seen as the 'servant' of functional goals of the organisation. In the 'manipulative mode', schools develop a caring ethos for the purpose of improving the performance of the organisation. Fielding (2007) draws from Ball's account of performativity in which teachers' actions are judged on their contribution to organisational performance and students are valued according to their contribution to the school's measurable outputs. This is summed up by: 'It is not so much what a school can do for its students, but what the students can do for the school' (Ball 1999 cited in Fielding 2007, p. 399). Fielding (ibid) suggests that such organisations increasingly achieve their ends by 'managerial reconstruction through the simulacra of care' (p. 400). Both students and staff in the high performance learning organisation are encouraged to enhance their contributions by 'carefully managed "ownership" of what others desire for you' (p. 400). The use of 'seductive technologies' such as learning styles, emotional intelligence, personal targets and so on form the framework for this approach. In this model, wellbeing is a tool through which to achieve other ends.

The Person Centred Learning Community Here in the 'intentional mode' the functional is for the sake of the personal, and in its most developed form, the 'expressive mode' the functional is expressive of the personal. In the intentional mode, the emphasis is on adapting the traditional arrangements to extend the school's focus to that of a learning community. Hence pedagogical approaches are adopted that foster motivation, creativity, negotiation between pupils and teachers and innovative approaches to assessment etc. Thus a careful eye is kept on external requirements such as curricula and examinations, but a genuine attempt is made to deliver this within a framework which values the individuals as people and is more open to 'holistic purposes and pursuits'.

In the 'expressive mode' of person-centred learning community, 'Teaching subjects and getting results are only justifiable insofar as they help young people to become better persons' (Fielding 2007, p. 403). Studies are therefore only undertaken if they are thought to be interesting and worthwhile. Fielding emphasises the importance of students' and teachers' communications being at the heart of the organisation (not simply limited to formal consultation) and giving rise to a 'communally situated individuality'.

5.3 Using Fielding's Typology to Examine the Discursive Relationships Between Learning and Wellbeing

Fielding's distinction between the personal and the functional aspects of schooling resonate with the themes of this book – wellbeing and learning. Quite clearly learning is the main functional aspect of schooling, although in contemporary schooling this may include gaining knowledge and skills alongside learning to *be* a particular type of person. Wellbeing can be seen as a personal aspect of life that has recently migrated into the purview of education policy, and it is this claim by the state, to an expanded role in the private lives of children that draws attention to this as a topic of study. Of course learning cannot be exclusively viewed as 'functional' any more than health and wellbeing can be seen to be solely 'personal', but the overlap between the personal and the functional, which Fielding emphasises in his discussion of Macmurray's work allows this to be used as a basis for enquiry.

The models of schooling identified by Fielding are predicated on a different relationship of means and ends between the personal and the functional aspects of school life. Similarly, the discursive relationships between learning and health and wellbeing invite examination of their means and ends. In the high performance learning organisation wellbeing is *for* learning and in the person-centred learning community learning is *for* wellbeing. However, when these two are examined in the context of the five discursive themes of wellbeing it becomes evident that the two types of relationship draw from different understandings of wellbeing. This is explored below.

5.3.1 Wellbeing for Learning in the High Performance Learning Organisation

The high performance learning organisation is geared towards socialising children in ways that maximise the achievement of the goals of the school. Learning in this context is deemed to be successful if it helps the school to meet the measurable targets by which its performance is judged. In this context the emotional wellbeing of children is valued because it is thought to lead to better performance. Indeed, proponents of emotional literacy have developed persuasive arguments pointing to the benefits *for the school* of a focus on childhood wellbeing.

Writing before these ideas were widely adopted in policy, Weare (2004) commented that concepts of mental health were not well understood in schools, and moreover that schools often found it difficult to see the relevance of mental health to their main business of learning and teaching. Consequently, she set out to convince schools of the relevance of emotional literacy to their work. She argued that the benefits of emotional literacy included improved school standards as indicated by better atmosphere, more effective learning, improved behaviour, higher levels of attendance and better results for students and schools. She also suggested that attention to emotional literacy would help schools to meet the policy requirements for inclusion (as measured by reductions in exclusions), due to improvements in behaviour. In the longer term she claimed this would benefit the workplace and also bring advantage to society through better communities and more active citizenship. Although this must be read as a publication purposefully written to convince policy actors and school managers, it is nonetheless notable that improvements to the emotional lives of individual children (i.e. mental health and wellbeing as an intrinsic good) did not feature in her justifications for introducing emotional literacy into schools. Weare's enthusiasm for emotional wellbeing as a tool for better outcomes remains undimmed as demonstrated by a more recently published international systematic review examining the evidence of a link between mental health promotion and 'problem prevention' in schools (Weare and Nind 2011).

Hence the high performance learning organisation seeks to enhance learning by concentrating on an individualised feelings and would work with children to develop personal attributes such as resilience, self-esteem, and motivation. This is delivered through an ethos of 'care'. The staff in a high performance learning organisation would pay attention to many of the aspects of care that were outlined in Chap. 4, but to Fielding (2004) this is an 'instrumental use of trust' in which opportunities for listening to students are managed so staff only hear what they want to hear. Community feeling is encouraged only as an instrumental tool to greater efficiency. This resonates with Noddings (2005a) who maintains that discussions which are guided by adults to reach particular (foregone) conclusions do not constitute truly caring dialogic interactions.

Fielding (2011) points to the ways in which schools may adopt a discourse whose lexicon echoes a more caring approach whilst following an outcome driven agenda. For example, the term 'personalisation' is widely used in contemporary schooling and may be thought to indicate a concern for the person. On the contrary, he argues pedagogical approaches that go under the banner of personalisation focus on the autonomous learner on his/her individual trajectory encouraged only to seek personal improvements in attainment. Fielding contrasts this with a similar term, personalism, which locates the child at the heart of a nexus of relationships through which the individual learns and develops. Similarly, many of the aspects of personhood can be appropriated for the purposes of organisational performance.

Thus Fielding (2007) suggests that in a policy environment that valorises social capital, 'collaboration and networking' are the 'new delivery agents of higher performance' which 'are likely to usher in a new era of increasingly sophisticated, increasingly dubious forms of influence and control' (p. 394). More recently he commented 'our understanding of the nature and importance of community as the means and end of human flourishing has been opportunistically co-opted and betrayed by the increasingly visible hand of neo-liberal market economics' (Fielding 2012, p. 687).

This can be interpreted as a contemporary example of 'governmentality' (Foucault 1991) whereby the subjectivity of children is subtly manipulated to align with policy objectives, through the exercise of 'bio-power' (Foucault 1979) or 'power over life'. Bio-power involves a form of regulatory control whereby macro-level policies are enacted through micro-level interactions (in this case the relationships between teachers and children in schools). At an individual level, the objectives of the state are converted into chosen behaviours by the process which Foucault (1977) refers to as discipline. Discipline, he describes as a policy of coercion and surveillance that produces the economically useful, self-regulating 'docile body'. However, the type of self-regulation that is being encouraged in the high performance learning organisation goes beyond the management of the physical body to the manipulation of feelings and shaping of personal subjectivity, so that children are not only told what they should do, but also guided in their feelings and relationships (Furedi 2004). This can be viewed as the present-day face of the potentially coercive nature of 'care' that has long been delivered through statutory bodies (Hendrick 2005).

Rose (1999) refers to this governmental focus on personal feelings as the 'therapeutic turn'. He argues that whilst the formation of self, in a neo-liberal society, is a personal project, personal subjectivities are also a vital element in the networks of modern society. The state needs mechanisms to control the subjectivity of the citizens in order that they make personal choices that support the activities of society as a whole. Echoing Foucault, Rose (ibid) suggests the governance of subjectivity, 'has taken shape through the proliferation of a complex and heterogeneous assemblage of technologies' (Rose 1999). The 'caring' strategies identified by Fielding in the high performance learning organisation, such as the focus on emotional literacy, attention to pupil voice, personal learning styles and individualised learning plans are examples of such 'technologies', giving the appearance of pupil centred strategies, but underpinned by the purposes of school performance.

Rose (ibid) refers to technologies which work on personal emotions as 'therapies'. Their focus is highly individualised with an emphasis on self-management. Terms such as 'enabling', 'emancipation' 'empowering' are used to describe their function, which is, he argues, to restore the failing individual to the autonomous condition required to navigate the individualised pathways of choice. Life, Rose suggests, has become a skilled performance in which the self must learn social skills, social competence, how to conduct conversations and manage relationships. The focus is on 'doing' relationships rather than 'having' relationships (Fielding 2011).

In the high performance learning organisation, the focus of emotional literacy is to 'fix' individual children, rather than paying attention to the structural difficulties that might be faced by families and communities (Coppock 2010).

In summary, the high performance learning organisation has a neo-liberal orientation, and an agenda of performativity. Measurable learning outputs are its key goal. Wellbeing is the servant of learning outcomes. Wellbeing is conceptualised as a psychological state in which children are sufficiently emotionally stable to engage with learning and have developed strategies to help them cope in the face of difficulty. Emotional health and wellbeing is supported by a carefully controlled ethos of 'care', in which the outcomes of discussions and debate will serve to align personal subjectivity with the aims of the school. Childhood agency would be supported insofar as it encouraged 'responsibilisation' (Watson et al. 2012) and adherence to the adult agenda. Community is important in that it may be a useful tool to enhance efficiency, but the overall orientation is individualistic. The support offered to children in this type of school would fall short of Noddings' (2005a) categorisation of care based on a truly dialogic relationship.

5.3.2 Learning for Wellbeing in the Person Centred Learning Organisation

The person centred learning community is based on a notion of human flourishing that resonates with the philosophical discourses discussed in Chap. 3. The purpose of education in this model is to widen opportunities for children to lead lives they have reason to value both in the present and in the future. The focus moves from an inward looking analysis of emotions to an outward looking view of how to live well in the world.

Although Fielding does not use the terminology of the Capability Approach there is evident resonance between the purposes of a person-centred learning community and the concepts of the Capability Approach. Both offer an alternative to neo-liberal models of human capital by challenging the notion that the worth of a person can be measured through his/her economic activity (Walker 2006). Both reject atomistic ideas of humans as isolated beings, seeking only to further self-interest, but instead emphasise the reciprocity between community and individual wellbeing, with a focus on the heterogeneity of individuals (Sen 1992) and rich personhood (Giovanola 2005). Both hold similar positions on means and ends. Where Fielding insists that the functional should serve the personal, Sen (1999) insists that the purpose of economic development should be to enhance opportunities for wellbeing, hence they are both rejecting an ideology in which the mechanisms of the free market take precedence over human flourishing. However, both also acknowledge the potential for confusion between means and ends, given that they are both fundamental aspects of human existence. Thus Fielding (2007, p. 394) says:

> *Ends and means must be inextricably linked; the means should be transformed by the ends by which they are inspired and towards which they are aiming.*

Similarly, the Capability Approach holds that the distinction between human ends and means must be constantly reiterated, because humans are the primary means of productivity, as well as the recipients of the benefits (Alkire 2005).

Importantly, in the context of this study, the person-centred learning community shares with the Capability Approach a belief in the intrinsic value of education for the benefit of the individual. At the most fundamental level, the Capability Approach endorses both health and education as basic capabilities that a person requires in order to lead a life they have reason to value (Dreze and Sen 1995). Lack of opportunity to participate in education and inadequate access to health care are described as 'unfreedoms', or factors that reduce a person's capability to lead a life they have reason to value. Not, only that, but unfreedom in health, such as disease or starvation can result in unfreedom in education i.e. failure to attend or benefit from schooling. For this reason, school based health and nutrition programmes form an important strand of the Education for All movement in developing countries. Thus, a distinction can be made between capabilities required to participate in education, and capabilities gained through education (Wood and Deprez 2012).

As an economist, Sen has tended to refer to education as a basic capability, based on the uncritical assumption that it is a universal good. However, educationalists researching Capability would support Fielding's stance that not all of the activities that occur in the name of schooling necessarily promote human flourishing. For example, the damaging effect of abusive educational environments on young women in South Africa have been reported, demonstrating that some experiences, associated with educational institutions, can result in 'unfreedoms' rather than enhanced capability (Unterhalter and Walker 2007; Unterhalter 2003). Indeed, Sen (2006) himself has commented on the potentially divisive implications of the UK move towards increased provision of faith based schooling. In recent years researchers have begun to examine more specifically what form education for Capability should take. Walker (2006) suggests that in offering a 'compelling and assertive counterweight to dominant neo-liberal human capital interpretations of education' the Capability Approach allows us to ask a 'different set of questions' about education, its purposes and its delivery (p. 164). Moreover, Walker and Unterhalter (2007) argue that if the purpose of education is to enhance Capability, then anything which does not enhance the freedom to achieve wellbeing is not education, saying,

> *We thus need to engage the view that not everything counts as education, if we wish at one and the same time to argue that education expands human freedoms, agency and empowerment (p. 14).*

Sen's views also differed from contemporary educationalists in taking a future orientated view of education, saying that the main argument for compulsory education lies in the freedoms it will create for the child once adulthood is reached (Saito 2003). In the context of recent understandings of children's competency and their roles as active agents in the present and the future (Mayall 2002; Uprichard 2008), topical debates on education for wellbeing take into account the issues of children's functioning in the present alongside considerations of Capability in the future.

Literacy is viewed by Sen (1999) as a basic capability. Literacy can be seen as a functioning which provides the opportunity to participate in a wide range of social practices to maintain a literate social identity. Thus literacy functionings have wide ranging uses that open opportunities for wider freedom and choice (Maddox 2008). Nussbaum (2003) sees literacy as a central human capability necessary for a life worthy of human dignity. At its most fundamental level a basic education serves to enhance the opportunities for wellbeing.

Education for Capability, it is suggested should also encourage the development of a person who is capable of practical reason and able to form a conception of the 'good life' and be able to plan to live such a life (Bates 2007). Similarly, Flores-Crespo (2007) argues for an education in which the development of reason serves to 'better human beings in an ethical way and enrich our lives' (p. 48). For Nussbaum (2006) education involves enriching life by developing what she calls the 'freedom of the child's mind' (p. 392). She writes disparagingly of education programmes that are dominated by rote learning and internalising of information, suggesting that these approaches kill the freedom of the child's mind. Instead she proposes that if education is to enhance the capabilities of children it should encourage critical thinking (to examine oneself and one's traditions), world citizenship (binding human beings together by ties of recognition and concern) and narrative imagination (cultivated through expressive arts). Clearly, for Nussbaum (ibid) education for Capability addresses the twin issues of personal flourishing with the place of the individual in the local and international community.

Hence, there are important questions about curricular content and pedagogy in a person centred learning community, where learning is *for* wellbeing. If, as Fielding (2007) argues, the personal should be realised through the functional, or, even better, the functional is *expressive of* the personal, this should be reflected in the choices teachers make about learning and teaching. In this vein calls have been made, in the name of the Capability Approach for language teaching to encourage personal expression (Diehm and Magyar-Haas 2011), teaching of basic philosophy to encourage dialogic activity, enhance 'complex thinking', critique, imagining and connecting new ideas (Biggeri and Santi 2012) and for the arts to provide opportunities to reflect on personal experiences, attitudes and beliefs (Maguire et al. 2012). Similarly, Wood and Deprez (2012), identify features of a pedagogical approach to widen students' horizons, to prepare students for full participation and to empower students to engage authentically with diverse perspectives. Thus this approach is not aiming to add 'happiness lessons' to the curriculum, but is aiming to enhance wellbeing through the taught curriculum (Suissa 2008).

Where the Capability Approach may diverge slightly from Fielding's person-centred learning community, is in their views of the instrumental purposes of education. For Fielding, the person centred learning community can exist in two forms. The 'intentional mode' in which a commitment to 'wider human purposes' is operated alongside a purposeful attempt to adhere to the requirements of agencies such as examination boards, is seen as less well developed than the 'expressive mode'. The expressive mode would only justify teaching to support the achievement of qualifications if this could 'help the young people become better persons' (Fielding 2007, p. 403). By comparison Dreze and Sen (1995) are quite clear that the instrumental value of educational success in creating future freedoms is very important, and they would emphasise the usefulness of qualifications as tools in providing opportunities which in turn may enhance freedoms to choose a valuable life. Rather than dismissing economic considerations from their analyses, Dreze and Sen (ibid) seek to broaden the analysis, to view employability and economic gains as means rather than ends.

This account has demonstrated how the person-centred learning community resonates with the philosophical discourses of wellbeing, in particular the Capability Approach. However, it is evident that these overlap with discourses of care, as articulated by Noddings (2005a). The philosophical understanding of wellbeing as a life well lived locates people in deeply social situations placing values on responsive reciprocal relationships, based on true dialogue.

In summary, the person-centred learning community is informed by a welfare-liberal ideology which values personal choice and freedom, but sees the individual as deeply socially situated. It takes a philosophical view of wellbeing supported by an education that helps us to 'live a rich, full, abundant, joyous human life' (Macmurray 1931 cited in Fielding 2012, p. 678). Individuality is celebrated, and in part education serves to recognise and develop those things that are personally relevant. Unlike the high performance learning organisation, this approach is not seeking to manipulate children to enhance the measurable outcomes of the school, instead it is seeking to support each child to uniquely come 'into presence' (Biesta 2010, p. 80), or to 'learn to be human' (Macmurray 2012, p. 666) through creating a school environment predicated on true care and understanding in which they can flourish.

5.4 Using Fielding's Typology in Discourse Analysis

In distinguishing between approaches in which childhood wellbeing serves learning and other goals, and those in which learning is *for* wellbeing Fielding's typology has been very important in shaping the Critical Discourse Analysis conducted in later sections of this book. However, there are ways in which my analysis digresses from his work. For Fielding the unit of analysis is the organisation, as he uses his typology to categorise the managerial approach which predominates in different schools. In my work the comparison is not between schools, it is between discourses. Hence the value of Fielding's work to this study is the elaboration of two ideologically distinctive ways of viewing education, which utilise the relationship between learning and wellbeing in different ways. As my focus is not on the organisation, the terms 'high performance learning organisation' and 'person centred learning community' will not be adopted as analytical positions in this study. Instead, the book will explore the two discursive relationships: wellbeing *for* learning, and learning *for* wellbeing.

Whilst the terminology, at this point has become somewhat blander, the ideologies which frame these discursive positions are not forgotten. Also Fielding's ideas are a response to the English educational policy field which has, in recent years, veered strongly towards a neo-liberal style of school governance (Ball 2008). By contrast, this Scottish study is taking place in a policy context in which a historical commitment to social democratic values remains visible in policy, alongside the strategies to be competitive in the international knowledge based economy (Paterson 2003). Whilst Fielding suggests that, in the English context the two types of organisation are distinct, this study was designed to be open to the possibility that the two ideologies may be elided both in policy and in the interpretation of policy by individuals. Moreover, since the diversity of pupil experience in Scotland is more marked within schools than it is between schools (OECD 2007) it seemed likely that responses to issues of wellbeing may also differ within schools.

Therefore, rather than looking for large scale differences between schools, this study was interested in examining the ideological influences on policy, how these invoked the five discursive themes of wellbeing, and how these were recontextualised in the speech communities of teachers.

Importantly, this framework has brought criticality to the discussion of wellbeing discourses. In Chap. 4 the identification of five discursive themes of wellbeing (discourse of physical health promotion, discourse of social and emotional literacy, discourse of care, philosophical discourse of flourishing and emergent discourse of sustainability) were largely descriptive. This chapter has explored the political implications of the wellbeing policies in schools and begun to question issues of purpose and power.

5.5 Summary

The chapter discussed how the discourses of wellbeing can be invoked in the context of education for social justice, bringing a more critical perspective to the discussion of wellbeing. Drawing from Fielding (2007) it described how the relationships between the functional aspects of schooling (learning) and the personal aspects of childhood can be differently positioned to serve different purposes. Fielding distinguishes between a neo-liberal ‘high performance learning organisation’ which manipulates personal feelings and relationships to serve functional goals of performativity, and a welfare-liberal ‘person centred learning community’ which seeks to ensure all learning is personally fulfilling and meaningful. Fielding’s model is used to show how the discourse of wellbeing, may be appropriated to develop a manipulative type of ‘care’ to foster the types of learning that focus solely on the characteristics of human capital favoured in the job market. Conversely, learning can be seen to be the bedrock of human flourishing. This distinction provides an analytical basis for the Critical Discourse Analysis of Scottish policy that follows. However, unlike Fielding’s work, this study does not aim to compare schools, but rather is exploring discourses. It is not seeking to identify which of these discourses is in operation, but is instead looking to see where and how each of these is evident, and how they overlap.

Chapter 6
Discourses of Wellbeing in Scottish Policy

6.1 Introduction

The following pair of chapters examine the health and wellbeing policies in Scottish education. Whilst children's wellbeing is an international policy concern, Scotland's vernacular response provides an interesting context for this study as its policies are

J. Spratt, *Wellbeing, Equity and Education*, Inclusive Learning and Educational Equity 1, DOI 10.1007/978-3-319-50066-9_6

well developed and clearly articulated. Furthermore, in its framing of wellbeing as closely linked to learning it can be used to examine how wellbeing interacts with other aspects of school life. In focussing on Scotland I am not intending to take issue with a specific government and its policies, rather I am using a detailed and innovative set of documents published by the Scottish Government to illustrate the complexity of the discursive actions that can take place in the name of wellbeing.

As described in Chap. 2, policy is a powerful platform through which dominant groups shape the actions and perceptions of professionals. The success of policies depends in part on the way in which discourse is used in framing the policy, to invite buy-in from the participants. As noted earlier, wellbeing is an attractive term, and no doubt carefully chosen as a seemingly benign framework for an education policy that is imposing new responsibilities on teachers, reframing their role as professionals and re-shaping the relationship between the state and the child. This chapter will focus on how wellbeing is conceptualised in a particular policy context, drawing on the five different discursive themes identified in Chap. 4, namely the discourse of physical health promotion; the psychological discourse of social and emotional literacy; the discourse of care, the philosophical discourse of flourishing and the emergent discourse of sustainability. Chapter 7 will focus on the purposes to which these discourses are put in policy, as they are integrated into discussions of learning, in its broadest sense. These two chapters together will disentangle the 'milling mass' of discourses (Jager and Maier 2009) that coalesce around the notion of wellbeing in Scottish policy to reveal something of the ideological purposes to which they are put.

6.2 Health and Wellbeing in Curriculum for Excellence

In the 'Curriculum for Excellence' the two nouns 'health' and 'wellbeing' are used together, and the term 'health and wellbeing' operates in the singular (e.g. health and wellbeing *is* important) suggesting that it seen as a single concept. 'Health' is clearly defined, in the Schools (Health Promotion and Nutrition) (Scotland) Act 2007 (Scottish Government 2007a) using the World Health Organisation's (1948) definition of health as 'a state of complete physical, mental and social wellbeing and not merely the absence of disease or infirmity'. In other words, health is conceived as a state of wellbeing. As ever, it is less clear what is meant by wellbeing. Even in this well documented policy, the concept of wellbeing continues to be evasive.

Scotland provides a useful setting because the 'Curriculum for Excellence' mandates a responsibility to all teachers for health and wellbeing. Additionally, and to my knowledge uniquely, Scotland's policy explicitly links wellbeing to learning, calling the policy 'health and wellbeing across learning', whereby teachers are expected to consider the health and wellbeing of children at all times. This allows scrutiny of how the relationship between children's learning and their wellbeing is conceptualised in a contemporary educational context. It is this new focus on wellbeing as an integral part of school life that is the focus of this study.

A distinction is made in 'Curriculum for Excellence' between 'learning *in* health and wellbeing' and 'learning *through* health and wellbeing. The former could be re-phrased as learning *about* health and wellbeing and would include formal health education lessons, physical education classes, or learning about food and nutrition. The latter is a more diffuse term which alludes to the less tangible aspects of wellbeing that are addressed through the life of the school more generally. The focus of this study is not on those aspects of wellbeing that are taught as curricular subjects, it is on the more intangible aspects of wellbeing that are framed as the 'responsibility of all' in the context of 'health and wellbeing across learning'.

'Curriculum for Excellence' is communicated to Scottish educators through a vast and ever growing website that conveys information about all curricular areas from age 3–18, providing guidance on content, teaching approaches, and school life more generally. To select texts for analysis in this study, all papers relating to 'health and wellbeing across learning' were included, and so were generic documents that offered advice on learning and teaching, if they alluded in any way to wellbeing. The Scottish interagency policy, 'Getting it Right for Every Child' (GIRFEC) was included due to its close links to Curriculum for Excellence. The Scottish Government's Economic Strategies were included as they very clearly inform the direction of 'Curriculum for Excellence'. Finally, two local authority policies were included from 'City Authority' and 'Rural Authority' as these were the areas that interviewees were selected from (see Chap. 8).[1]

The following texts were scrutinised:

- Scottish Government's Economic Strategy. (Scottish Government 2007b, 2011, 2015).
- Key documents guiding the 'Getting it Right for Every Child' (GIRFEC) policy i.e. *Getting it Right for Every Child: Guidance on the Child or Young Person's Plan*, (Scottish Executive 2007) and both editions of *A Guide to Getting it Right for Every Child* (Scottish Government 2008, 2012).
- Selected papers from *The Curriculum for Excellence Building the Curriculum* series, namely: *Building the Curriculum 1: The contribution of curriculum areas* (Scottish Executive 2006) and *Building the Curriculum 4: Skills for learning, skills for life and skills for work* (Scottish Government 2009).
- The health and wellbeing webpage on Education Scotland's *Curriculum for Excellence* web-site and the pair of linked documents: *Curriculum for Excellence: Health and wellbeing across learning: responsibilities of all. Experiences and Outcomes* (Scottish Government n.d.a) and *Curriculum for Excellence: Health and wellbeing across learning: responsibilities of all. Principles and Practice* (Scottish Government n.d.b)
- The *Approaches to Learning* web pages in *Curriculum for Excellence*, specifically: Active learning; ICT in learning; creativity; outdoor learning; co-operative and collaborative learning; peer education; and Reggio Emilia.

[1] See appendix for a more detailed justification of the selection of texts.

- The Rural Council health and wellbeing strategy (2012) and The City Council health and wellbeing policy (2012). For reasons of anonymity their proper titles are not used.

A number of features make these texts different from the more traditional 'hard copy' documents that would have been used prior to the development of digital technologies. Firstly, by being housed on an extensive website the documents bring together technologies from different genres. In particular, the written documents are supported by visual images such as photographs or videos. The more substantial policy documents are supported by introductory texts and images on the web pages, which of themselves adopt a discursive position.

Secondly, the texts are not presented linearly, and the visitor to the website can move through it in any way (Fairclough 2003). Therefore, the policy cannot be designed around a sequential line of reasoning that all readers move through in the same order. Connections between texts are made by hyperlinks, which are themselves discursive acts. As will be shown, the location of health and wellbeing documents within the complex site, sends a message about the associations being made between them and other aspects of the curriculum. The sense of consistency is maintained across the multiple facets of the 'Curriculum for Excellence' website, by a deliberately repetitive vocabulary, rather than by progressively developing a coherent argument.

Thirdly, websites are subject to continual revision, without the need to leave a trace. Whole sections may be added, removed or re-located without notice. Documents can be moved and texts can be modified. Many entries on the website are undated, and it is not always made clear when updates are made, or how the policy has developed over time. This creates difficulties for the researcher whose careful reading of a text may be soundlessly rendered outdated. The sense of shifting sands whilst doing this work was disconcerting at times. Most the citations used are currently on the website at the time of going to press. Where I quote text is that has been recently removed, this will be identified.

6.3 Use of Language in the Policy Texts

Prior to discussion of the content of the specific policy texts it is perhaps useful to make a number of general observations about the use of language. The tone adopted in these documents, as in policy more widely is of a single (anonymous) institutional author, using an impersonal register. There is very limited use of intertextual referencing to external sources, to evidence or support the statements made. The United Nations Convention of the Rights of the Child (United Nations 1989) is cited as a key influence in 'GIRFEC' and in a number of places in 'Curriculum for Excellence'. The World Health Organisation is mentioned although in general terms rather than a specific citation. However, there is a great deal of internal inter-textuality as concepts and key phrases echo across the range of documents, sometimes overtly referenced, but usually not.

Mostly the statements made are assertions, with little accompanying evidence. Justification is made through repetition rather than argument. Writing does not tend to flow in a series of connected sentences and paragraphs, to build up a case, but instead tends to jump from one idea to another often without any obvious connection (possibly indicating a more diverse set of authors than the tone of the text would imply). Take, for example the following paragraph from Building the Curriculum 1, p. 6:

> ***Developing responsible citizens***
> *Children and young people need to learn to respect and value other people and to develop an understanding of their beliefs and feelings. This will help them to develop positive relationships, promote equality and fairness and counter discrimination. Developing young people's awareness of healthy diet, activity, positive relationships and risks to health lays important foundations for their future life, including parenting. From an early age, children and young people can develop an understanding of how their actions and decisions are affected by and affect others, recognising how important it is to behave in ways that can have a positive effect on other people and the environment.* (Scottish Executive 2006, p. 6)

On first inspection this paragraph seems eminently sensible; the vocabulary is positive and conveys ideas that are generally thought to be 'good', to which most teachers or parents would instinctively ascribe. However, a closer inspection identifies a lack of reasoning in the paragraph. It begins with the assertion that children and young people *need* to learn to respect and value others, and follows with another assertion that this *will* help them to develop positive relationships. This is offered as 'taken for granted' or 'common sense' rather than evidence based, or clearly argued policy. The purpose of demonstrating this is not to take issue with the veracity of these particular statements, but to demonstrate how the language of these policies operates.

Moving to the third sentence there is a sudden shift in content. Without qualification the topic moves from the focus on equality and fairness (in sentence 2) to address diverse topics of diet, activity, positive relationships, health risks and parenting together in one sentence. Returning to the theme of responsibility to others, the final sentence points to the social effect of individual behaviour, then at the very end, suddenly the three words 'and the environment' appear. This disjointed writing style which constantly moves from one topic to another, forming tenuous links between key concepts of 'Curriculum for Excellence' is the norm, and this will be evident in many of the quotes used later.

Fairclough (2003) describes a method for distinguishing between a paragraph which is a series of assertions and a paragraph that in which an argument has been constructed. That is to try and re-order the sentences. In an argument the sentences follow each other, and would not make sense in a different order. In the paragraph above sentence 1 and 2 form a pair, but otherwise the statements made could be put in any order.

The overall effect of this style of writing is to leave no room for other viewpoints. In the example above there is no acknowledgement that some people's view or activities may not merit respect, or that children may need to learn to distinguish between people who they trust and people who they do not trust – instead the focus is exclusively on the positive aspects of harmonious relationships. In examining this paragraph my purpose is not to debate this issue in particular, but to point out how the policy rhetoric fails to acknowledge the existence of other voices.

6.4 The Discursive Representation of Wellbeing in Scottish Policy

The following sections will look in detail at the how the five discursive themes of wellbeing are invoked in Scottish policy. It will demonstrate how the most dominant discourses are operationalised models informed by the fields of social and emotion literacy and by physical health, which are, in turn, linked to a discourse of care. The discourse of sustainability and the educational discourse of flourishing are very largely missing from the documentation, and described as the quieter themes. These observations lead to an argument in the concluding section that the discourses of other professional groups have migrated into education policy and overshadowed educational discourses of wellbeing as flourishing.

6.4.1 Individualised Discourses of Wellbeing in Policy

This section will demonstrate how the psychological discourse of social and emotional literacy is prominent in 'Curriculum for Excellence' alongside a discourse of physical health promotion, and how these two are largely presented as an individualised model of operationalised acts.

The policy text 'Curriculum for Excellence: Health and wellbeing across learning. Responsibilities of all. Experiences and Outcomes' lists a set of attributes that it aims to foster in children (Scottish Government n.d.a). This document identifies those 'experiences and outcomes' which are the 'responsibility of all' (as opposed to the remit of subject specialists). It is here that the psychological discursive theme comes to the fore, accompanied by the discursive theme of physical health promotion. As these two themes often occur together they are discussed together here, but it will be evident that greater weight is placed on the former.

The experiences and outcomes are not intended to be formally taught, necessarily, but are considered to be desirable products of the educational experience as a whole. They are represented as endemic to all aspects of school life. It is here that the 'Curriculum for Excellence' characterises its conception of wellbeing most clearly. The document is written in the first person. The excerpt below is taken from the introduction to the document:

> I can expect my learning environment to support me to:
>
> - develop my self-awareness, self-worth and respect for others
> - meet challenges, manage change and build relationships

- experience personal achievement and build my resilience and confidence
- understand and develop my physical, mental and spiritual wellbeing and social skills
- understand how what I eat, how active I am and how decisions I make about my behaviour and relationships affect my physical and mental wellbeing
- participate in a wide range of activities which promote a healthy lifestyle
- understand that adults in my school community have a responsibility to look after me, listen to my concerns and involve others where necessary
- learn about where to find help and resources to inform choices
- assess and manage risk and understand the impact of risk-taking behaviour
- reflect on my strengths and skills to help me make informed choices when planning my next steps
- acknowledge diversity and understand that it is everyone's responsibility to challenge discrimination. (Scottish Government n.d.a, p. 1)

Very largely, this list presents an individualised view of health and wellbeing to be operationalised through the acquisition of skills. Use of the first person helps to convey the ontological individualism of the curriculum, although it is the norm for Experiences and Outcomes to be written in the first person across all areas of 'Curriculum for Excellence'. This may be intended to 'soften' the otherwise authoritarian nature of the proposed list. However, Priestley and Humes (2010) comment that although the consistent use of 'I', may be an attempt to convey a vision of the learner at centre stage, this can be seen as an artifice, as the language employed does not accurately represent that commonly used by pupils.

Fairclough (2003) suggests that the most distinguishing feature of a discourse is its vocabulary, or the way that it is 'lexicalised'. These itemised 'experiences and outcomes' draw very much from the language of emotional literacy as advocated, for example by Weare (2004). The atomistic vocabulary of emotional and social literacy runs across these items, with reference to 'self-awareness' 'self-worth', 'resilience' and 'confidence' alongside the development of 'skills' of understanding and management of self. Social interactions are portrayed as a performance: 'building relationships' and developing 'social skills'. Moreover, the individual liability for actions is clearly evident in the requirement to 'assess and manage risk'. Discourses of physical health promotion are also evident, again in the context of personal obligation. This would support the claim of Watson et al. (2012) who argue that the role of the state in childhood wellbeing focuses on 'responsibilisation of the individual'.

The experiences and outcomes articulated in the list above are largely normalising in their intention, prescriptive of 'appropriate' actions and feelings. Only some of the spectrum of human emotions are acceptable. Contemporary Scottish children for example are clearly not supposed to feel shy, or self-effacing and if they do so, not to express that feeling. Instead confidence and resilience are on the curriculum. In this way the curriculum is socialising children into a desired way of being by shepherding children's emotions in particular directions. The sense of universality, for example that a positive sense of self is always appropriate is questioned by Cigman (2012), who argues that, for example, that children who bully other children may not benefit by feeling pleased about their actions. Equally there are times when it is entirely normal, and emotionally healthy to feel 'negative' emotions, such as at times of bereavement. Failure to acknowledge a range of emotional states could be interpreted as stifling diversity, as only some ways of feeling are acceptable. Arguably, a focus on 'positive feelings', rather than encouraging children to be more in tune with their emotions could have the effect of silencing some those children whose lives do not induce these positive feelings.

The final bullet point, which sits uneasily at the end of such an individualised list, suddenly moves to a different discourse, linking wellbeing to the existence of an inclusive community, offering a fleeting acknowledgement that wellbeing may be communally situated as well as individualised. Possibly this hints at multiple authors involved in compiling such a list, and illustrates the way that policy production can suture different interests and perspectives in the same document (Rizvi and Lingard 2010), as it draws from different discourses.

The partner document 'Curriculum for Excellence: Health and wellbeing across learning. Responsibilities of all. Experiences and Outcomes' also offers definitions for teachers and other professional to help them understand relevant terminology. It is interesting to see what, the government believes, teachers need to know in order to understand their responsibilities. The page of definitions is quoted directly below:

> ***Resilience.*** *The development of resilience or coping skills is particularly important to young people as increasing numbers are struggling through school and life with social and emotional needs that greatly challenge schools and welfare agencies.*
>
> *A resilient child can resist adversity, cope with uncertainty and recover more successfully from traumatic events or episodes.*
>
> ***Mental wellbeing.*** *Mental wellbeing refers to the health of the mind, the way we think, perceive, reflect on and make sense of the world.*
>
> ***Mental health.*** *The World Health Organisation describes mental health as:*
>
> *'a state of wellbeing in which the individual realises his or her own abilities, can cope with the normal stresses of life, can work productively and fruitfully, and is able to make a contribution to his or her community.'*
>
> ***Emotional wellbeing.*** *Emotional wellbeing refers to recognising, understanding and effectively managing our feelings and emotions.*
>
> **Social wellbeing.** Social wellbeing refers to being and feeling secure in relationships with family, friends and community, having a sense of belonging and recognising and understanding our contribution in society.
>
> ***Self-esteem/Self-worth.*** *Self-esteem is a self-rating of how well the self is doing. It means:*
>
> - *the way we feel about ourselves.*
> - *the way we feel about our abilities.*
> - *the value we place on ourselves as human beings.*
>
> ***Physical wellbeing.*** *Physical wellbeing refers to the knowledge, skills and attitudes that we need to understand how physical factors affect our health. (Scottish Government*n.d.a, *p. 19)*

These definitions mainly reinforce the understandings of wellbeing as being a set of skills largely concerned with understanding and managing the self. The focus on resilience for children who are 'struggling through life' with 'social and emotional needs that greatly challenge schools and welfare agencies' raise an issue of social justice, by acknowledging the difficulties that some children face. However, the problem is discursively located in the emotional state of the child and the consequent difficulties this creates for schools and other agencies. Equally the solution appears to lie with teaching the child to resist adversity, rather than attempting to address whatever may lie behind the problem. In the guise of resilience, individual health and wellbeing is being invoked as the solution to a wider problem. By attempting to address the problems that children face by working on the psyche of the child, and his or her ability to cope, Morrow and Mayall (2009) would argue that policy is ignoring the structural causes of such problems and failing to consider the politics of childhood. As agued by Wilkinson and Pickard (2010), we cannot address the harms caused by societal inequalities through 'mass psychotherapy' to reduce emotional vulnerability, we need to reduce inequality itself.

As noted earlier, physical health is mentioned, but not as prominently as psychological wellbeing. However, physical wellbeing appears not to be associated with a being in a state of good health, (for example being physically fit). Instead it is defined as possessing the knowledge and skills and attitudes to *understand* how to be healthy. Hence it is framed as a choice. By informing children and young people about their health, it becomes their responsibility, resonating with the observations of other writers (Burrows and Wright 2007; Johnson et al. 2013; Moore 2012).

However, the single entry that related to social wellbeing in this context does move away from the usual analysis of 'social skills' and instead we see here a richer view of the complexity a web of relationships with friends, family and community, leading to a sense of 'belonging' and, making a 'contribution', with no delineation of what that might be. This sits a little uneasily in the personalised list above, but provides an intertextual link to the discourse of care that will be considered in the next section.

6.4.2 Discourse of Wellbeing as Care in the Interagency Policies

The discursive theme of care is the dominant theme in the interagency policy guidance, *Getting it Right for Every Child* (GIRFEC) (Scottish Government 2012). There is an interesting shift in the understanding of wellbeing in this document compared to 'Curriculum for Excellence' in spite of the close relationships claimed between the two policies. In answer to the question 'What is Getting it Right for Every Child?' the following statement is made:

> *It's a consistent way for people to work with all children and young people. It's the bedrock for all children's services and can also be used by practitioners in adult services who work with parents or carers* (Scottish Government 2012, p. 6).

Shortly afterwards, under a side heading 'What Getting it Right for Every Child means for practitioners' the following bulleted points are offered:

- *Putting the child or young person at the centre and developing a shared understanding within and across agencies.*

- *Using common tools, language and processes, considering the child or young person as a whole, and promoting closer working where necessary with other practitioners* (Scottish Government 2012, p. 6).

Thus a sense of holism is evident in the reference to the child or young person 'as a whole', and in the notion of the 'child at the centre' of a joined-up interagency approach to care of children. We can also see in these excerpts an objective of shared understanding, consistent approaches and a common language between different professionals. It is therefore notable that 'wellbeing' has been selected as the ostensibly shared concept around which the policy of care is framed, reinforcing Ereaut and Whiting's (2008) suggestion wellbeing is a notion to which different professional groups will readily ascribe.

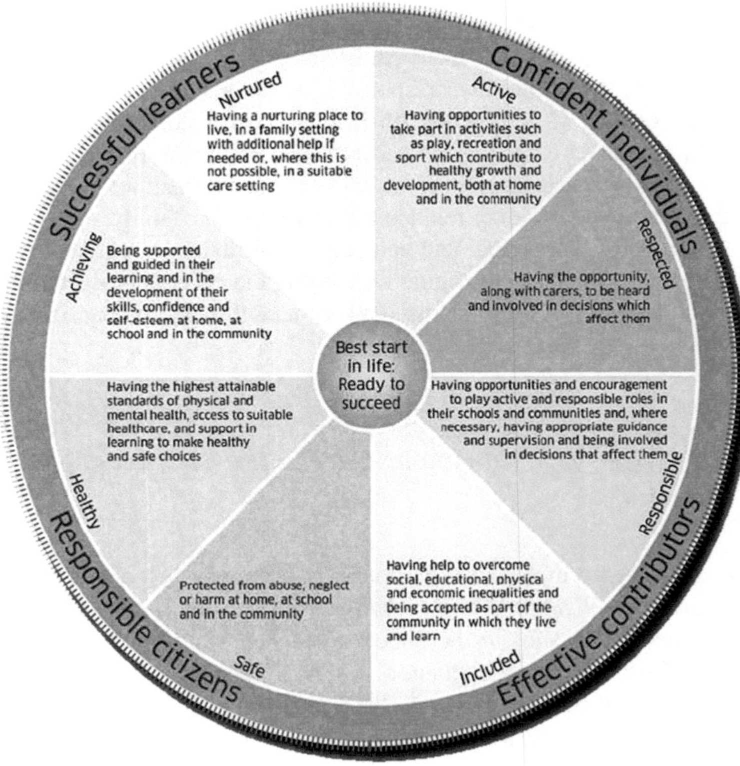

Figure GIRFEC's wellbeing wheel (Scottish Government 2012, p. 10)

GIRFEC addresses childhood wellbeing by focusing on the duty of professionals and other adults towards the care of children. It conceptualises wellbeing in terms of development. The policy identifies eight 'indicators of wellbeing' which are described as 'the basic requirements for all children and young people to grow and develop and reach their full potential' (Scottish Government 2012, p. 10). The indicators are: safe; healthy; achieving; nurtured; active; respected; responsible and; included (referred to collectively with the acronym SHANARRI). The wording on each sector of the model is phrased in terms of the adult responsibility in conferring the rights, for example 'having help to overcome' difficulties, being 'protected from abuse', being 'guided and supported in learning' or 'having opportunities to take part in activities such as play'. This model locates deficits in the environment rather than the child, and sees the role of professionals in working together to ensure that a nurturing environment is in place. It is evident that in the interagency policies, that the conceptualisation of wellbeing differs in emphasis from the educational policies.

Wodak (2009) points out that iconography is an important aspect of discourse. The format of the 'wellbeing wheel' conveys an image of completeness and an authority that may not exist in written text. It effectively becomes a 'model'. It gives the mixed message, cautioned by Noddings (2005b) of a holistic understanding (the circle representing the 'whole child'), operationalised through a list of discrete attributes of wellbeing and provisions to be assessed by professionals. In particular, this model seems to indicate that the role of professionals is to assess situations against the eight indicators, and then 'plug gaps' where there appears to be a deficit of care.

The wellbeing indicator that has most resonance with education is 'achievement'. GIRFEC advises monitoring children for signs of development that would be in line with their age group or other expectations. As a model primarily designed to guide interagency responses when children are deemed to be experiencing difficulties, it tends to discuss education in terms of expected norms and progress, rather than content and pedagogy, as shown in the following excerpt:

> *Education and social milestones need to be recorded. Personal learning plans and other educational records should provide evidence of what has been achieved and what supports are needed or being provided for. Is the child's progress with formal education in line with expectations?* (Scottish Government 2012, p. 18).

Again we see an agenda of socialisation, or fitting in with the norm, with little heed taken to the element of flourishing that might be associated with a good education.

Although the interagency discourse of care in GIRFEC differs in emphasis from the education policies, links between the two policies are made in places. GIRFEC is recontextualised most clearly in the policy text: 'Curriculum for Excellence: Health and wellbeing across learning: Responsibility of all: Principles and Practice' (Scottish Government n.d.b) for example in the following statement, which juxtaposes care with behaviour management:

> *Children and young people should feel happy, safe, respected and included in the school environment and all staff should be proactive in promoting positive behaviour in the classroom, playground and the wider school community* (Scottish Government n.d.b, p. 1).

Although GIRFEC is not directly mentioned in this document the diagram of the 'wellbeing wheel' is copied in its entirety, accompanied by the assertion that it represents a 'shared vision and common goal'. (Presumably the vision is 'shared' between government departments). Without further elucidation, nor an indication of its source, there is an implicit assumption that GIRFEC is familiar to readers, and underpins work on health and wellbeing.

In a section entitled: *Health and wellbeing across learning: the responsibilities of all* practitioners the policy sets out how all adults working with children contribute to the health and wellbeing of children. Very largely this invokes the discursive theme of care as shown in the excerpt below:

> *Everyone within each learning community, whatever their contact with children and young people may be, shares the responsibility for creating a positive ethos and climate of respect and trust – one in which everyone can make a positive contribution to the wellbeing of each individual within the school and the wider community. There are many ways in which establishments can assist young people. These include peer support, buddies, breakfast or lunch clubs, safe areas, mentors, pupil support staff and extended support teams.*

Here the vision of care and support is articulated specifically for the school context, providing examples such as peer support lunch clubs, pupil support staff and so on. The emphasis lies on professionals working to establish 'open, positive, supporting relationships', allowing 'children to feel listened to', suggesting something of the dialogic relationships of care, to which Noddings (2012) *alluded.*

However, a significant point, in terms of the focus of this book, is that very largely this caring discourse is applied to the ethos and environment of the school, rather than to teaching and learning. In the document there is just one mention of the importance of pedagogies for effective learning offering a fleeting suggestion that learning may be an important feature of childhood wellbeing.

6.4.3 Links Between Discourse of Care and the Discourse of Social and Emotional Literacy

From the discussion above it is clear that the three key documents of GIRFEC, *Curriculum for Excellence Health and Wellbeing: Principles and Practice* and *Curriculum for Excellence Health and Wellbeing Experiences and Outcomes* each serve different purposes, but also speak to each intertextually. In GIRFEC a discourse of care dominates. In the Principles and Practice, the discourse of care is contextualised specifically in the school setting and the environment is set for the development of the emotional, social and physical health competences referred to as Experiences and Outcomes. In this way the discourses of care are linked to the psychological discourses, for example in the following quotation:

> *The mental, emotional, social and physical wellbeing of everyone within a learning community should be positively developed by fostering a safe, caring, supportive, purposeful environment that enables the development of relationships based on mutual respect* (Scottish Government n.d.a, p. 2).

Similarly, the discursive themes are woven together in the following statement which until recently could be found on, the *Curriculum for Excellence* Health and Wellbeing website.[2]

> Where young people feel included, respected, safe and secure and when their achievements and contributions are valued and celebrated, they are more likely to develop self-confidence, resilience and positive views about themselves

The complexity of the connections between the discursive theme of care, in terms of the school ethos, the development of relationships and the psychological attributes of individual children is evident in the following paragraph taken from *Curriculum for Excellence: Building the Curriculum 4: Skills for learning, skills for life and skills for work.* In the following paragraph we see the discursive theme of care interweaving with the psychological discursive theme, both of which, it is suggested are important for learning:

> *Health promotion is not just about encouraging children and young people to eat well and to exercise; it encompasses a much broader holistic approach. At the heart of health and wellbeing is the capacity to form and sustain good personal, social and working relationships. Such relationships underpin successful learning, as they are the key to motivation and engagement with the values and ideas of Curriculum for Excellence. When children and young people have good relationships, they are more likely to feel self-esteem and confidence with regard to their learning, to show resilience when faced with personal challenges, and to show respect for others. Schools and their partners in whatever setting have a vital role to play in supporting young people as they develop resilience, the motivation to face and learn from setbacks and the ability to make mutually supportive relationships. An ethos of trust, integrity and democracy, which values all engaged in the care and supervision of children and young people, will help foster an environment of personal, social and emotional development* (Scottish Government 2009, p. 17).

This is a good example of the way in which policy texts jump between concepts, weaving together discourse fragments with intertextual links to statements made elsewhere. Here we are told that the 'ethos of trust, integrity, democracy' fosters wellbeing, and that the heart of wellbeing is the 'capacity to form and sustain good personal, social and working relationships'. These relationships are not simply valued for their own sake. They give rise to desirable psychological characteristics in individuals such as 'self-esteem and confidence'. Moreover, good relationships 'underpin successful learning', and are the 'key to motivation and engagement with the values and ideas of *Curriculum for Excellence*'. Hence the personal relationships of children are being construed as a vehicle to achieve other policy goals. This will be further discussed in the next chapter which considers how wellbeing is used in the educational environment.

---

[2]Interestingly, these exact words can now be found in a Curriculum for Excellence behaviour management leaflet, supporting the argument made in the following chapter that health and wellbeing often serve other purposes of schooling (Scottish Government 2013).

6.4.4 The Quieter Themes – Sustainability and Flourishing

The discursive themes of flourishing and sustainability are both rare within the 'Curriculum for Excellence' health and wellbeing policies. However, the documents scrutinised in this study also included a suite of texts collectively entitled 'Approaches to learning'. Like their partner documents, these papers also privilege discourses of wellbeing as social and emotional literacy, physical health promotion and care. Importantly, they do also, in a minor way, illustrate the use of the discourses of sustainability and flourishing in policy. Although these discourses do not form the main thrust of the documentation, they do slip in, in a small number of places, sometimes using a different style of writing, or lexicon to the other policy texts, suggesting different authorship. They suggest there is a space for other possible understandings of wellbeing in education.

In the booklet 'Curriculum for Excellence: Outdoor Learning', (Scottish Government 2010) some references are made to the discursive theme of sustainability. Illustrated with photographs of healthy looking children in waterproof jackets, (foregrounding wellbeing as experiential) the paper seeks to emphasise the benefits of time spent out of doors to the health and wellbeing of children. Moreover, this document moves beyond the portrayal of wellbeing as a set of skills of emotional management. On the introductory section of the web page it says:

> *Curriculum for Excellence offers opportunities for all children and young people to enjoy first-hand experience outdoors, whether within the school grounds, in urban green spaces, in Scotland's countryside or in wilder environments.*
>
> *Such experiences inspire passion, motivating our children and young people to become successful learners and to develop as healthy, confident, enterprising and responsible citizens.*

The use of the word 'passion' is unusual in the policy texts scrutinised here. It draws from a different vocabulary to that of emotional literacy. Passion could not be seen as a 'skill' or a 'disposition' – it is an emotional response to an experience. All too soon passion is linked to the more familiar mantra of *Curriculum for Excellence*, such as successful learners, responsible citizens, but nonetheless it offers a different perspective, if only for a moment. Interestingly, the sustainability policy is seeking to justify itself through a link with wellbeing, but the converse is not true. To find discursive links to sustainability it was necessary to look beyond the health and wellbeing policies themselves. It could be argued that this link was made by the authors of the outdoor learning policy in the way identified by Ereaut and Whiting (2008) who showed actors with different purposes sought to link their work with wellbeing as a signal that there were 'good things' going on. The word 'wellbeing' can be used in a fairly general way in order to increase the attractiveness of another agenda.

The philosophical discourse of flourishing is also absent from the health and wellbeing policy itself. However, it is most evident in the few paragraphs included in the *Approaches to Learning* webpage devoted to Reggio Emilia. Here the webpage summarises the approach to early development that has emerged from the work in the Italian town of Reggio Emilia. Drawing from educational theorists Bruner and Vygotsky it sets out the advantages to this approach in terms of improved learning. Later on the article includes the following paragraphs:

> *This is a child who is driven by curiosity and imagination, a capable child who delights in taking responsibility for his or her own learning, a child who listens and is listened to, a child with an enormous need to love and to be loved, a child who is valued.*

This is an account that captures the philosophical idea of wellbeing achieved through the opportunities offered to live an active, interesting life. The emotional lexicon is not the self-orientated language of emotional literacy, it is an outward facing vocabulary of 'curiosity', 'imagination' taking 'delight' in learning and needing to 'love and be loved'. Although the term health and wellbeing is not invoked in this context, we see a vision of a child who is flourishing. However, this sits strangely with the health and wellbeing policy as a whole and must be seen as an indication of different authorship of different parts of the curriculum, whereby a different vision can quietly slip in to a small corner of the documentation. It also points to the fluidity of discourses within the curriculum and opens a space within 'Curriculum for Excellence' for eudaimonic considerations of wellbeing.

6.5 Conclusions

In drawing from the discourses of health promotion, emotional literacy and care, emanating from professional fields of medicine, psychology and social care, this policy is an example of bricolage (Ball 2007), whereby bits and pieces are borrowed from different sources. It is clear that certain representations of wellbeing are favoured. In examining the professional and academic sources of the discourses we can see that education policy has been influenced by branches of psychology, by social care and by physical health promotion. As children's services have shifted over recent years to be seen as interagency partners, rather than discrete silos, the discourses of other professional groups have migrated into education policy, under the guise of health and wellbeing. Many authors, including myself (Spratt et al. 2006), have, since the turn of the twenty-first century urged schools to learn lessons from other child professionals such as social workers, education psychologists and health workers in order to go beyond simply delivering education, to also paying attention to wider needs of children. Where schools were previously perceived, in some cases to view children exclusively in terms of their learning, there was, justifiably a strong call for greater attention to be paid to the emotional lives of children.

However, it now appears the discourses of other agencies have overshadowed educational discourses in discussions and conceptualisations of wellbeing in schools. As argued in Chap. 4 the philosophical understanding of wellbeing as flourishing, or leading a life you have reason to value (Sen 2009) is the most educational of the discourses. Here the value of a life is understood, not by inward looking analysis of emotions, but of outward looking considerations of opportunities and freedoms to understand and pursue a life of value. In Scotland's 'Curriculum for Excellence' the voices of other professional groups appear to have overshadowed the educational voice in the conceptualisation of wellbeing.

In adopting a discourse of wellbeing as a set of physical, emotional and social skills that can be taught, children are construed as malleable creatures (Gasper 2004), whose feelings, subjectivities and their very *being* are available as a resource for government use. Moreover, it conveys an individualised and rather pessimistic view of contemporary life, whereby the response to difficulties is to look inwards and change the self, through coping, developing resilience, and managing emotions, instead of looking outwards to explore the possibilities of making changes (Furedi 2005). Children are taught to believe that life will be tough and they had better learn how to cope, instead of learning that the world is full of multiple possibilities to explore. Wellbeing is conceptualised as 'well-feeling' rather than 'well-living' (Gasper 2004).

In very large measure the Scottish government uses the concept of wellbeing to offer a vison of what sort of citizens it would like. By framing wellbeing as individual attributes it paints a picture of self -reliant, confident, children in control of their emotions, who responsibly weigh up risk to inform their sensible choices. Through the platform of education of policy, the government is using the discourse of wellbeing to shape very personal aspects of children and future adults. In so doing it is using the health and wellbeing policy to socialise towards a new emotional norm, favouring a particular type of person. The following chapter will examine how this supports and is supported by other aspects of schooling and why it might be happening.

6.6 Summary

I have demonstrated how discourses of wellbeing emanating from other professional and academic groups have been adopted in Scottish education policy, overshadowing a more educational discourse of wellbeing as flourishing. Wellbeing is mainly characterised in terms of social and emotional literacy, linked to a discourse of care. A discourse of physical health promotion is also present, although less prominent. The discourse of sustainability within the context of wellbeing is a quieter theme in the documents although, this is an emerging discourse that will no doubt become more prominent. Although the discourse of flourishing through leading a valuable life is very quiet in these papers, there is a just a glimmer of hope that there is space in 'Curriculum for Excellence' for this interpretation.

In these documents childhood wellbeing is conceptualised as an individualised way of being. Its focus lies on an inward looking gaze as young people learn to understand and manage themselves in ways which allow them to present in socially acceptable ways. It draws from discourses of physical health promotion as children are encouraged to recognise and responsibly navigate risk. By distancing considerations of childhood wellbeing from the socio-political factors that impinge on children's lives, the discourses of wellbeing can serve to divert attention towards within-child solutions.

Chapter 7
Interactions Between Wellbeing and Other Purposes of Schooling in Scottish Policy

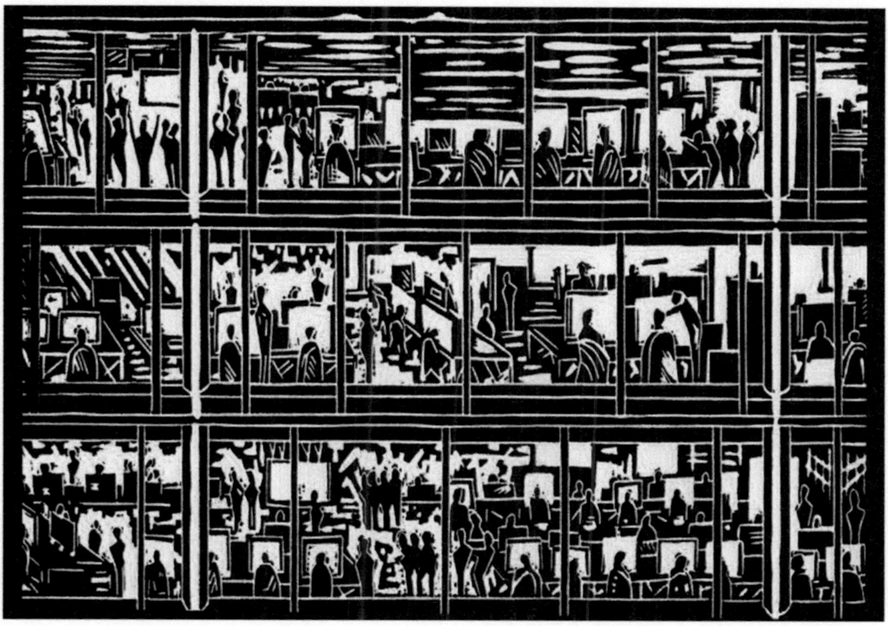

Building on the argument in Chap. 6 that wellbeing in Scottish education policy is conceptualised mainly as a set of individualised skills of emotional and social self-management, responsibility and risk awareness, linked to a discourse of care, I will now examine how this conceptualisation of wellbeing plays out in relation to other aims of schooling. Chapter 2 showed how education can be seen to have composite purposes, such as serving the nation's market economy, supporting children to understand and develop their individual strengths and interests and fostering sense of democratic fellowship. These different views of education give rise to different understandings of the role of the school in the endeavour for equity and social justice.

We saw in Chap. 5 how schools can manipulate the discourse of wellbeing to support different ends. Drawing from Fielding (2007) it became evident that schools can, in some circumstances, use seeming child-centre language to frame policies and

J. Spratt, *Wellbeing, Equity and Education*, Inclusive Learning and Educational Equity 1, DOI 10.1007/978-3-319-50066-9_7

practices whose purposes were to support the school in meeting its own targets of performance more than they were to do with the emotional care of the child. If the purposes of schooling are solely to feed the mechanisms of getting children into work, then the discourse of wellbeing is subsumed to those goals. If, on the other hand schooling has a more social democratic purpose of development and fulfilment of people who thrive because of their learning, then the notion of wellbeing becomes more complex.

I will now continue the Critical Discourse Analysis of Scottish policy to examine where and how wellbeing is discursively invoked to serve other purposes of schooling and where and how wellbeing is portrayed as the outcome of learning. In this section, where the purposes of policy are scrutinised, issues of power emerge, as we consider what the state may be trying to achieve through the policy discourse of wellbeing.

7.1 The Purpose of the Scottish Curriculum – The 'Four Capacities'

Any understanding of the policies and practices within contemporary Scottish education, must take into account the 'four capacities'. When the 'Curriculum for Excellence' was introduced, it marked itself as different from the previous national curriculum (the 5–14 Curriculum), as it was no longer simply driven by attainment. Moving from a model of learning that focussed solely on measurable outcomes, the new curriculum was interested in the process of learning and saw educational benefits as much wider than simply attainment. The overarching purpose of the Scottish lay in the 'four capacities', as explained in the quotation below:

> *The purpose of the curriculum is encapsulated in the four capacities – to enable each child or young person to be a successful learner, a confident individual, a responsible citizen and an effective contributor* (Education Scotland n.d.)

In the light of concerns about of the poverty-related 'attainment gap' in Scotland (Sosu and Ellis 2014) recent developments aimed at refocussing the curriculum have re-introduced attainment as a key policy concern (Education Scotland 2016) and this may have the effect of narrowing the understanding of the term 'successful learner'. Nonetheless this change has been made within the existing framework of 'Curriculum for Excellence', with the four capacities continuing to be the overall stated purpose of the curriculum. It is evident that in Scotland, education is not only learning *about* things (knowledge), or learning *how to do* things (skills), it is learning *how to be* a particular type of person. The education system in Scotland broadened its remit into development of the characters of its young citizens. This has been important in shaping the health and wellbeing policies.

The introduction of the four capacities has been welcomed as a giving greater freedom to teachers in moving away from attainment driven teaching (Priestley 2010), allowing teachers to focus on broader issues and consider the development of the child as a whole. It has also been criticised as an attempt to build human capital by seeking to develop attributes associated with potentially productive workers (Lingard 2008). Either way, the state has widened its remit in terms of shaping its young citizens, so that it dictates something of who they are as well as what they know. Whilst the terms 'successful learners', 'confident individuals' responsible citizens' and 'effective contributors' have become something of a taken-for granted mantra in Scottish schools, there seems to have been little questioning of the right of the government to intervene so directly in shaping the characters of children. Nor has there been any explanation on the part of the Scottish Government as to what their purposes are. We are left to surmise.

Character education is not, of course unique to Scotland. Arthur (2005) argued that the UK's New Labour government was responsible for a resurgence in interest in shaping the character of citizens, arising from concerns that a decline in influence of the church left a moral vacuum in the population. However, he argued that the moral virtues espoused by government align closely with their aspirations for economic and community engagement. Schools were cited as the centre piece of such policies. More recently, Ecclestone (2012) has identified how such behaviour change is supported by focussing on the emotions of children. By adopting a discourse of psychological wellbeing, such as emotional regulation, resilience, and stoicism, she argues that moral development is shaped through policy without the need for discussion of the values or purposes that lie behind it. It is to the purposes of the Scottish Government that we now turn, starting with the Economic Strategy.

7.2 Economic Strategy

The economic policy frames all other policies in Scotland, and provides an important backdrop to the educational policies. It also demonstrates how the 'four capacities' are invoked in the economic strategy. At the time of writing the Scottish Nationalist Party is in power in the devolved Scottish Parliament and has been since 2007. It has published three iterations of the Economic strategy in 2007, 2011 and 2015. In each case the core purpose of government is clearly stated:

> *Since 2007, this Government's central purpose has been to create a more successful country, with opportunities for all of Scotland to flourish, through increasing sustainable economic growth. This remains the Government's ambition to which all our efforts and actions are directed and is at the core of our Economic Strategy* (Scottish Government 2015, p. 4)

The Scottish Government, like all other countries seeks economic growth, but it also aims to use the fruits of the economy to benefit the whole population, not only the industrialists. It clearly states the twin pillars of increasing competitiveness and reducing inequality. Arguably, here we can see the both the welfarist and the market strategies sitting side by side. Whilst some commentators have commented on the evident tensions between these two aspects of Scottish policy (Lingard

2008), Scotland's First Minister, Nicola Sturgeon claims, in the Foreword to the Economic Strategy that 'delivering sustainable growth and addressing long-standing inequalities are reinforcing – and not competing – objectives' (Scottish Government 2015, p. 5). However, Scott and Mooney (2009) argue that anti-poverty strategies in Scotland are inextricably linked to neo-liberal economic strategies. Equality is seen as connected to the mainstream economy, with work rather than re-distribution as the main anti-poverty strategy.

Education has two key roles in the economic strategy: firstly to provide the type of workforce that a competitive country needs and secondly to tackle inequalities in opportunity to participate in the labour market by addressing what is known as the 'attainment gap'. To this extent, education is called upon to address both of the key concerns of the Scottish government by ensuring the employability of its young citizens. In describing the economic ambitions of the government term 'human capital' is used:

> *Going forward, our investment in the human capital – the education, skills and health – of the people of Scotland will be a central focus of our actions to deliver Scotland's Economic Strategy.* (Scottish Government 2015, p. 39)

Education in this context is seen as entirely economic in its purpose and its contribution to social justice is seen as enhancing employability.

Interestingly, the latest economic policy, under the leadership of Nicola Sturgeon focuses mainly on educational attainment, and makes no mention of the 'four capacities', whereas the previous version of the strategy (under Alex Salmond) stated:

> *The four capacities at the core of Curriculum for Excellence – successful learners, confident individuals, responsible citizens and effective contributors – will enable our young people to develop the attributes, knowledge and skills they will need in the modern workforce* (Scottish Government 2011, pp. 61–62).

This statement further supports a reading of the understanding of education as human capital development. Whilst there are signs that the latest Scottish leadership may be returning to a focus on educational attainment, contemporary health and wellbeing policy was drafted with the four capacities at centre stage.

7.3 Discursive Links Between Wellbeing and Learning

Drawing from Fielding's (2007) analysis of the different relationships that can exist between the functional and personal aspects of schooling this section examines the discursive connections that link learning to wellbeing in Scottish policy. In particular, the analysis identifies where wellbeing was construed as serving learning or where, alternatively learning was represented as supporting wellbeing. Additionally, the analysis sought to identify how the five discursive themes examined in Chap. 6 were invoked in these relationships.

Broadly, these fall into two camps, that will be organised as wellbeing serving learning, (which dominate the policy) and learning for wellbeing. The second category, learning for wellbeing is further divided into learning about health and wellbeing; linking achievement to psychological wellbeing; and learning for flourishing.

In discussing these relationships, the analysis also seeks to uncover the ideological positions that are masked by the appealing language of wellbeing. This section will suggest the policy of wellbeing may not be as benign as it appears on the surface.

7.3.1 Wellbeing Serving Learning

By far the most common discursive use of wellbeing was to represent it as a prop to other purposes including learning, the development of the four capacities, and other desirable character traits. Alongside this health and wellbeing is represented as serving employability.

The health and wellbeing webpage in Curriculum for Excellence opens with the statement 'Good health and wellbeing is essential for successful learning and happy lives for children and young people'. Although it is encouraging to see the mention of 'happy lives' in this context the focus of the remainder of the policy is on learning. Throughout the documentation the phrase 'health and wellbeing is central to learning' repeats several times with the focus on social and emotional wellbeing. The idea that the purpose of wellbeing is to support the main school focus, i.e. learning is also phrased in many different ways for example:

> *'How we feel about ourselves and others influences everything we do. It has a huge impact on learning and success in life'.*

Here we can see that wellbeing is not valued in its own right; in the school context it serves a specific purpose. Children who are thought to be in possession of the 'skills' of psychological wellbeing are portrayed as likely to do better at the things that schools want them to do. By attending to aspects of wellbeing that may foster better learning the school appropriates aspects of personhood for other purposes. This exemplifies Fielding's (2007) suggestion that schools may manipulate the personal aspects of children's lives for the benefit of the functional aspects of schooling (learning).

Wellbeing is not only invoked in the context of learning in general, it is also specifically linked to the development of desirable attributes. Hence it not only supports learning *about* things (knowledge) or learning how to *do* things (skills) it also supports learning how to *be* a particular type of person. For example, the role of health and wellbeing in supporting the development of personal characteristics is evident in *Building the Curriculum 1: The contribution of the curriculum areas* (Scottish Executive 2006) which sets the scene for many of the subsequent documents in the 'Curriculum for Excellence'. This text offers a justification for health and wellbeing as the 'responsibility of all', by asserting:

> *Learning through health and wellbeing promotes* ***confidence***, ***independent thinking*** *and* ***positive attitudes and dispositions****. Because of this, it is the responsibility of every teacher to contribute to learning and development in this area* (Scottish Executive 2006, p. 15).

The first sentence posits health and wellbeing *for* the development of 'independent thinking' alongside desired 'attitudes and dispositions'. It is followed by a non-sequitur which falls short of providing an argument for the universal responsibilities. These paired sentences are widely quoted in other 'Curriculum for Excellence' texts, both local and national, as a kind of default rationale for many health and wellbeing policies. The wellbeing policies aim to shape children's personal growth and development in a direction that produces particular types of people. A socialising function of the health and wellbeing policies can be seen in their attempt to normalise certain behaviours and attributes in young people.

A causal link is also made between positive wellbeing and development of the 'four capacities' – the character traits that lie at the core of the 'Curriculum for Excellence' (successful learner, confident individual, responsible citizen and effective contributor). The diagram of the SHANARI wheel (See Fig. page 78) shows the four capacities running around the perimeter of the eight-spoke wheel, implying a close link between wellbeing and the four capacities. The causality of the relationship between the two is identified in the following paragraph which suggests that wellbeing supports the development of the four capacities:

> *The wellbeing wheel (also) shows the connections between children and young people's wellbeing now, and their well-becoming in the future. The Scottish Government and its local government partners ...... have an ambition that all Scotland's young people will be successful learners, confident individuals, effective contributors and responsible citizens.* ***This depends very much on how well they have been supported to develop their wellbeing.*** *All agencies in touch with children and young people must play their part in making sure that young people are healthy, achieving, nurtured, active, respected, responsible, included and, above all, safe'* (Scottish Government 2008, p. 10).

This can be interpreted as an example of the 'therapeutic turn' (Furedi 2004) in education, whereby professionals are charged with directing the emotional lives of children in an attempt by the state to manipulate the population into particular types of people. The role of policy in advocating this version of health and wellbeing resonates with the arguments of Rose (1999) who talks of governing through the 'science of the soul'. The school based intervention in health and wellbeing can be construed as a 'technology' in the governance of subjectivity, aiming to enable the 'self' to navigate through the individualised pathways of schooling and contemporary society. In Rose's (ibid) view life has become a skilled performance in which the self must learn social and emotional skills, in order to meet socio-political obligations of the 'good citizen'.

Moreover, the link between children's wellbeing in the present and their future is made explicit through discussions of employability. For example, *Building the*

Curriculum 4: Skills for learning, skills for life and skills for work, makes the following statement:

> *Skills in personal learning planning and career management, working with others, leadership and physical co-ordination and movement all relate closely to health and wellbeing as well as to enterprise and employability* (Scottish Government 2009, p. 18).

This suggests that the 'skills' to which the label health and wellbeing have been attached serve to support a future trajectory that supports employability. A further example of the discursive link between health and wellbeing to employability was evident in early versions of GIRFEC documentation where a hyperlink to the Government's Economic Plan was provided alongside the statement that: 'The delivery of the [GIRFEC] outcomes will support the overall strategy of growing the Scottish economy in order to develop opportunities for all' (Scottish Government 2008, p. 6).[1] Most evidently, it links GIRFEC's focus on childhood wellbeing to the economic aims of the government.

There is a very strong message repeated across the documents that the personal (wellbeing) should serve the functional (learning). Wellbeing is not valued intrinsically, it its place in the curriculum is argued for in terms of the contribution it makes to the wider purposes of schooling. Therefore, one possible interpretation is that the 'Curriculum for Excellence' health and wellbeing policy is designed to develop human capital. Contemporary accounts of human capital include not only the curricular knowledge and skills acquired from education, but extend to the 'entire ensemble of capacities embodied by individuals' (Sellar and Lingard 2013). This 'capitalisation' of people extends to the management of relationships, as this makes it easier for people to work together in the pursuit of economic success (Gillies 2011). Consequently, in cultivating the attributes and dispositions of the self-reliant resourceful individual characterised by 'health and wellbeing', which enhance learning and underpin the four capacities, which in turn are elided with 'skills for work' this could be interpreted as an arm of the neo-liberal project.

However, this sits uneasily with the Scotland's traditional claim to more welfarist purposes. An alternative explanation is that the impression created by this policy was not intended. Perhaps the policy was drafted in this way to convince teachers of the value of childhood wellbeing. Weare (2004) argued that teachers do not necessarily recognise the relevance of mental health and wellbeing, and may be reluctant to accept responsibilities in this area. Possibly the repeated assertions that wellbeing is helpful to learning was intended to persuade a disinclined teaching profession to be more attentive to the emotions of children. Or possibly this is an example of policy making as 'muddle', as policy makers adopted and abridged from other sources, including the Social and Emotional Aspects of Learning (SEAL) programme that was widely used in England at the time (Hallam 2009), they uncritically adopted a new set of discourses, which they sought to incorporate seamlessly into the new curricular structure.

---

[1]Interestingly the reference to the economic strategy is omitted in the updated *Guide to Getting it Right for Every Child* (Scottish Government 2012).

My own knowledge of the policy community leads me to feel disinclined to believe that the overt human capital message conveyed by the policies was a deliberate act. This may be an example of a discourse 'acting behind the backs of the subjects' as policy makers sought to suture government economic plans with more welfarist aims of health and wellbeing. Apple (2006) points the inadvertent role played by the professional and managerial bureaucrats in education, many of whom would view themselves as politically left learning, who, in the name of efficiency, carefully draft and evaluate policies which ultimately serve the neo-liberal state. Perhaps the bureaucrats in this case were unaware of the agenda they were supporting. Whatever the original intentions of these policies, it is clear that it is possible for the discourse of wellbeing to be manipulated to serve purposes other than the best interests of children. Regardless of provenance, the Scottish case illustrates how policies of wellbeing cannot be assumed to be benign and how governments can use soft sounding language to normalise the emotions of children and socialise towards state endorsed outcomes.

7.3.2 Learning for Wellbeing

Whilst the discourse that portrays wellbeing as a prop to support other activities is by far the most common link that is made between learning and wellbeing, there are places in the policy where the link runs the other way and learning is portrayed as supporting wellbeing. The functional can also be seen as portrayed, less frequently as servant to the personal. These relationships can be seen in three formats, which will be considered in turn: learning *about* wellbeing; achievement enhancing psychological wellbeing; learning for flourishing. In these manifestations different discursive themes of wellbeing become evident, and there are hints of other ideological understandings of learning.

7.3.2.1 Learning About Health and Wellbeing

All teachers in Scotland are charged with some responsibility for health and wellbeing, so learning about health can take place either formally and informally in any setting. Whilst the remit of this book excludes scrutiny of, for example the physical exercise curriculum or food and nutrition lessons, it does include those aspects that permeate school life through the policies of 'health and wellbeing across learning'. The features of health and wellbeing that are the 'responsibility of all' are clearly itemised in the 'Experiences and Outcomes' (Scottish Government n.d.a). These might be addressed as cross curricular opportunities, extracurricular curricular activities or the more diffuse undertakings of the so called 'hidden curriculum'. The attributes that teachers are expected to foster in their pupils, is an example of learning for wellbeing, although the teaching and learning may be very informal and indirect.

Unsurprisingly, the discourses of wellbeing that are utilised here are those that used to define wellbeing as outlined in Chap. 6, i.e. psychological discourses of social and emotional wellbeing and the discourse of physical health promotion. I return to these discourses briefly here, simply to underline that they are associated with learning – being a desired outcome the health and wellbeing policy. The specific learning outcomes are detailed as bulleted points in three sections: mental and emotional health and wellbeing; social health and wellbeing and; physical health and wellbeing. Each section is populated with a long list of desirable attributes, marked as the 'responsibilities of all'. To avoid cherry picking from the extensive choice of learning outcomes, the first two from each section are used as illustrations below. For example, the mental and emotional health section begins with:

> *I am aware of and able to express my feelings and am developing the ability to talk about them.*
>
> *I know that we all experience a variety of thoughts and emotions that affect how we feel and behave and I am learning ways of managing them* (Scottish Government n.d.a, p. 2).

Here we have an individualised conception of wellbeing as understanding, expressing and managing emotions.

The social health and wellbeing section opens with:

> *As I explore the rights to which I and others are entitled, I am able to exercise these rights appropriately and accept the responsibilities that go with them. I show respect for the rights of others.*
>
> *I recognise that each individual has a unique blend of abilities and needs. I contribute to making my school community one which values individuals equally and is a welcoming place for all* (Scottish Government n.d.a, p. 3).

These are a series of operational actions by which the individual makes him/herself socially acceptable. They set the rules of engagement for social interaction in the school setting and as such they portray social life as a performance in conformity (Rose 1999). Whilst this section makes clear that individuals benefit from their social relationships it falls short of depicting the unique and complex relationships that take place between closely interacting human beings.

This point was vividly illustrated at a professional development event I attended in which a national policy actor introduced teachers to the, then, new health and wellbeing policies. Discussions turned to how the policy would be appraised; how would teachers know that they had been successful in fostering social wellbeing? The reply came that teachers and schools would never be expected to assess whether children had any friends, but instead they would be expected to demonstrate that children knew what the advantages of friendship were and understood how to behave respectfully to each other. From the perspective of this policy actor, the very thing that most people value most dearly about being human, having friends, was not the point, but the knowledge and performance of social skills was.

The physical health and wellbeing section starts with the following two outcomes:

I am developing my understanding of the human body and can use this knowledge to maintain and improve my wellbeing and health.

I am learning to assess and manage risk, to protect myself and others, and to reduce the potential for harm when possible (Scottish Government n.d.a, p. 3).

Again we can see an individualised notion of health as self-management and responsibility. The learning outcomes portray health and wellbeing as a set of skills that can be taught in schools. It corresponds with Ereaut and Whiting's (2008) notion of wellbeing as an 'operationalised list'. It describes a series of personal attributes that feed directly into the discussions of human capital the previous section.

7.3.2.2 Linking Achievement to Psychological Wellbeing

Another way in which the learning is construed as supporting wellbeing is through the positive effect of success on feelings of self-esteem. This is a discursive strand portraying learning *for* psychological wellbeing. This is evident in the GIRFEC documentation. Of the eight 'indicators' on the SHANARI wheel, only one relates to learning, and this is labelled 'Achieving' with the following elucidation:

Achieving: Being supported and guided in their learning and in the development of their skills, confidence and self-esteem at home, at school and in the community (Scottish Government 2012, p. 10).

The main link made between learning and wellbeing in the first edition of A *Guide to Getting it Right for Every Child* (Scottish Government 2008) is not the value of knowledge per se, or the enriching experience of learning, it is the outcome of *achieving,* which in turn is valued as a means to improve self-esteem and confidence. Thus doing well, is construed as important emotionally, linking to the psychological discourses of wellbeing as an emotional state.

Referring to the GIRFEC indicators of wellbeing, the following statement appears on the 'Curriculum for Excellence' Health and Wellbeing webpage. This has been cited earlier, but it is reiterated here to demonstrate a different point.

Where young people feel included, respected, safe and secure and when their achievements and contributions are valued and celebrated, they are more likely to develop self-confidence, resilience and positive views about themselves.

This statement points to the psychological benefits gained from 'achievements' which are 'valued and celebrated', suggesting that it is the salutation of the learning outcome which promotes wellbeing. The motivation for learning is extrinsic, as the most important issue here is praise for the achievement. In a sense the argument has become circular; the child who is praised for learning will feel good about themselves, which will in turn encourage further learning. This is a socialising mechanism for encouraging children to engage with whatever learning is on offer. The intrinsic value of learning, the extent to which the child found it relevant, interesting, enriching or satisfying, that could be called the 'joy' of learning

(Griffiths 2012) is ignored. The discourse of flourishing through learning was rare in the documentation, and will be discussed below.

7.3.2.3 The Rare Discursive Strand: Learning for Flourishing

Throughout the health and wellbeing documentation in 'Curriculum for Excellence' the discursive strand of learning *for* flourishing was very quiet. However, there were glimpses of a discourse of learning for flourishing in some of the 'Approaches to learning' web links. Overall, references that could be interpreted as learning for flourishing were fragmentary but where they did occur there was some juxtaposition with outdoor learning. For example, in *Building the Curriculum 1: The contribution of curricular areas* (Scottish Executive 2006), when discussing the role of health and wellbeing in the development of the four capacities, the following sentence appears (see Sect. 6.7.1):

> *Through their learning in health and wellbeing, children and young people can have opportunities to engage positively in experiences that are fun, enjoyable, exciting and challenging in a variety of settings including the outdoors* (Scottish Executive 2006, pp. 14–15).

In a single sentence, linguistically unconnected with the remainder of the document, a vision of children actively involved in learning which is 'fun, enjoyable, exciting and challenging' offers a brief glimpse of children flourishing in their education, or learning *for* wellbeing. Outdoor learning as a vehicle for wellbeing is echoed elsewhere in 'Curriculum for Excellence', conveying a more complex inter-relationship between learning *about* health and wellbeing, being physically active in a healthy environment (fresh air) and simultaneously flourishing through meaningful learning.

> *Learning outdoors can lead to lifelong recreation. Activities such as walking and cycling which are ideal for physical and emotional wellbeing contribute to a healthier Scotland.* (Scottish Government 2010, p. 5).

> *'All aspects of the curriculum can be explored outside. The sights, sounds and smells of the outdoors, the closeness to nature, the excitement most children feel, the wonder and curiosity all serve to enhance and stimulate learning.'* (Scottish Government 2010, p. 10).

Thus, in the outdoor learning section of 'Curriculum for Excellence' we see some evidence of learning which is designed to enhance health and wellbeing, and which is taking a wider view than simply a set of skills to support other aspects of life. A description is offered of children feeling 'excitement', and 'wonder and curiosity' in the natural environment, displaying a type of emotional vocabulary that is missing in the main bulk of the government policy. And we see hints of an emotional benefit from 'interacting with greenspace', again an example of improved wellbeing as a *result* of the learning experience.

Similarly, the Health and Wellbeing policy from Rural Council used examples from case study schools to demonstrate a much more complex relationship between learning and health and wellbeing than simply good health as a prop for effective learning. Consider the following account of one school's sustainable garden:

> *At xxx School the creation of a sustainable garden lies at the heart of our health and wellbeing vision. Our garden provides a living, outdoor learning context within school grounds. It is an outdoor classroom where children's learning becomes real. Children can make connections, understand processes and apply new skills all in a meaningful, motivating and fun learning environment.*
>
> *The garden will provide a focus for health and wellbeing activities over the coming sessions. This will range from planning, planting and managing the garden, to harvesting the produce. The produce itself will be used within the school kitchen to provide a range of fruit and vegetables to the children. We plan on providing local residents with affordable vegetable boxes, while the children themselves will be involved with cooking. The garden is not just for growing, it will provide an eco-system on our doorstep, where children can experience and develop an understanding of both the plants and the animals that live there.*

In this account of one school's work we can see the process of learning framed as part of the understanding of health and wellbeing. Here 'learning becomes real' as children are involved in 'making connections, understanding processes and applying new skills' in a 'meaningful, motivating and fun learning environment'. We can also see the skills and knowledge that are part of this process being framed as part of the development of health and wellbeing. Whilst the curricular content of this project overlaps with the health and wellbeing experiences and outcomes, in respect of food and nutrition, it is much wider, overlapping with science, ecology, citizenship and other areas. Health and wellbeing is not conceptualised simply as skills of self-management to support other aspects of life. Here we have a notion of health and wellbeing deeply interwoven with meaningful learning, and a recognisable discourse of learning *for* health and wellbeing that is wider than simply learning *about* health and wellbeing.

Finally, we return to the example of flourishing through learning that can be found in a very short article, housed in the *Approaches to learning* web page. The author's voice in this document takes a distinctly different tone to the remainder of 'Curriculum for Excellence' as it describes a vision of childhood development as follows:

> *Rather than seeing the child as an empty vessel waiting eagerly to be filled with knowledge, Reggio educators believe strongly in a child with unlimited potential who is eager to interact with and contribute to the world. They believe in a child who has a fundamental right to 'realise and expand their potential'.*
>
> *This is a child who is driven by curiosity and imagination, a capable child who delights in taking responsibility for his or her own learning, a child who listens and is listened to, a child with an enormous need to love and to be loved, a child who is valued.*

This is an account that captures the philosophical idea of education as vital to the way a person lives in the world. It is through learning that this child understands and fully interacts with the world around him or herself. The child's emotional need 'to love and be loved' is not separated from the 'curiosity and imagination' that is involved in learning. It is *through* learning that the child is able to fully develop. This is an account of flourishing through learning, resonating with Macmurray's

(2012) suggestion of 'learning to be human'. Moreover, this vision of childhood development also draws from a discourse of care, based on dialogue between adults and children:

> *It is an approach where the expressive arts play a central role in learning and where a unique reciprocal learning relationship exists between practitioner and child.*

In this account learning involves emotions; the two are not separate. This is not the child conveyed elsewhere in the 'Curriculum for Excellence' whose emotions need to be brought under control before learning can take place. This is a child whose wellbeing is enhanced through learning, in a context of care. So, although rare, there were a few hints of learning for flourishing. indicating that there is space within the curriculum for thinking in that way, although this does not articulate very clearly with the dominant discursive strands of the health and wellbeing policy.

It seems therefore that there may be some opportunity for interpretations of flourishing through learning in the 'Curriculum for Excellence', but that this is located in a different silo from the health and wellbeing policy. This study is not claiming that the 'Curriculum for Excellence' does not allow for flourishing through learning, but it does claim that discourses of health and wellbeing are not invoked in that way. The important contribution that teachers uniquely can bring is virtually absent from the discursive treatment of health and wellbeing, whether by accident or design.

7.4 Summary

Overwhelmingly in Scottish policy health and wellbeing is portrayed as a set of skills of self-management that serve other purposes. Wellbeing is seen as a means through which other ends can be achieved. The 'Curriculum for Excellence' repeatedly asserts that health and wellbeing is a prerequisite of learning, that it supports the development of 'positive' dispositions and that it underpins the characteristics of the 'four capacities'. Moreover, health and wellbeing is seen to be part of the 'skills for learning, skills for life and skills for work'. The health and wellbeing agenda is discursively linked to the Government's economic agenda. Suggesting that a focus on individual health promoting activities and emotional management serves to produce a more robust workforce. In Fielding's (2007) terms, the personal is used to support functional goals.

The converse relationship of learning, as important for wellbeing (or the functional serving the personal) is less prominent. Learning *about* health and wellbeing is the most obvious link in this direction, but this refers to the development of knowledge and skills, which in turn will support other aims. The notion of learning *for* childhood flourishing, (where wellbeing was the end purpose of education), was less common. Occasional references to high quality learning experiences offered discursive links between pedagogy and wellbeing. However, there was little suggestion that acquisition of new knowledge could, of itself, could support eudaimonic wellbeing. In the context of the other two curricular themes deemed to be the 'responsibility of all', literacy and numeracy, it was clear that wellbeing was portrayed as a necessity for these to develop, but any suggestion that becoming more literate and numerate might be important for children to flourish was missing.

Overall the Scottish policy documentation gives an overwhelming impression of the appropriation of children's health and wellbeing by a neo-liberal, human capital agenda, in the model of the high performance learning organisation (Fielding 2007). In largely overlooking the educational discourse of learning for flourishing, it has managed to work the other themes together to provide a consistent message of childhood wellbeing serving other objectives, and invites an interpretation of a deliberate appropriation of young personhood into the human capital project.

Yet, there is a dissonance between this and the welfarist aspirations to which Scotland lays claim (Paterson 2003). Another reading of this could be that somehow, at the interagency discussion table the intrinsic value of education was simply overlooked as an aspect childhood flourishing. If the policy was worked up through the messy processes of borrowing, amending, consulting, and appeasing different interests, then it is possible that the oversight is the consequence of policy as 'muddle' rather than manipulation (Lindblom 1959). It may be the case that in designing the policy, England's Social and Emotional Aspects of Learning programme (e.g. see Hallam 2009) was 'borrowed' from extensively and hence the discourses of another national policy community migrated into Scotland without too much critique.

One can also imagine that the inter-agency discussions that were involved in drafting the document took place in a professional environment in which the concept of wellbeing had naturalised or taken for granted as a 'good thing', with little critical discussion of purposes. As the concept of wellbeing was sutured on to the education policy, and links made where ever possible to 'smooth over' connections between different interests, there may not have been any overt intention to harness childhood wellbeing to the plough of to the global marketplace. Nonetheless, regardless of intent of the individual involved, the effect remains the same. This demonstrates how ideologies that serve the purposes of dominant groups can disguise their purposes under the mantle of common sense, so that the individuals may not be aware of the discourses to which they ascribe (Fairclough 2010).

At the same time, hidden away in little corners of the 'Curriculum for Excellence' website, were some suggestions of flourishing through learning. This is in indication of the multiple interests that co-exist in the enormous project that is 'Curriculum for Excellence', and these leave the door open for alternative understandings of the relationships between learning and wellbeing. As will be seen next, some teachers did indeed find other ways of conceptualising this relationship.

Chapter 8
The Discursive Gap: Interpretation of Policy by Professionals

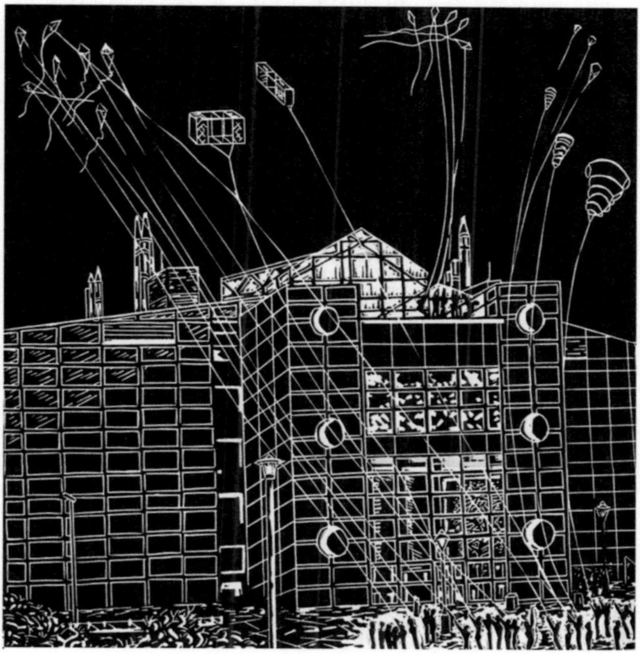

It is widely acknowledged that when policy moves from the written format to being enacted by policy users, it is subject to change as individuals interpret the policy in the light of their own experiences and perceptions of their role (Maguire et al. 2015; Singh et al. 2013). This is what Bernstein (2000) referred to as the 'discursive gap' where policy may be interpreted and enacted in ways which were not entirely congruent with the intentions of the policy makers. Hence it was important for this study to explore how policy actors and teachers understood their role as educators called on to enact the health and wellbeing policy. Twenty-five interviews were conducted with nine policy actors and sixteen teachers.[1] In the chapter that follows

[1]Details of the methods can be found in the appendix

J. Spratt, *Wellbeing, Equity and Education*, Inclusive Learning and Educational Equity 1, DOI 10.1007/978-3-319-50066-9_8

the findings from interview data will be presented and discussed, demonstrating where discourses echo, recontextualise or differ from those that that were evident in policy.

8.1 The Study Participants

Policy actors were identified who held strategic roles in the delivery of policy in schools. At a national level key informants were identified working in both education and health. One policy actor from a children's voluntary sector organisation was also included. Schools were selected from two local authorities. At local education one education policy maker was included from each of the two education authorities participating in the study. It had been the intention to include one interview with the individual responsible for school health in each local health board. However, in one health board this post was vacant, so no interview could take place. The table below introduces the policy actors and their roles. Pseudonyms were used for all study participants.

Pseudonym	Organisation
Stephen	Scottish Government, Learning Directorate
Helen	NHS Health Scotland, Policy Development Officer
Susan	Education Scotland
Margaret	Education Scotland
Simon	Scottish Children's Charity
Hilary	Scottish Health Promoting Schools Unit (formerly)
Harry	City Local Authority, Quality Improvement Officer
Nigel	Rural Local Authority, Quality Improvement Officer
Gillian and Mary (job-share partners)	City Local Authority and NHS (co-funded), Health Improvement Officers

In each local authority, which have been called Rural Local Authority and City Local Authority, one primary school and one secondary school were selected. The selection of schools was informed by the local authority representatives (Harry and Nigel) who were in a position to advise which schools were actively developing their work in this area. It was important for a study of discourse that the interviewees were involved in recent developments in wellbeing in schools so they would, hopefully, feel able to talk quite freely in the interview. In each local authority one primary and one secondary school were included in the study. The four schools can be characterised as:

- City Academy. Inner city school serving multiple areas of deprivation. 915 pupils. The school had achieved the status of a 'School of Ambition' based on its health promoting activities.
- City Primary School. Inner city school serving area of deprivation. 221 pupils. The school had achieved level 2 of the UNICEF Rights Respecting School award.

- Rural Academy. Serving rural town and surrounding areas. Mixed socio-economic intake. 1122 pupils. The head teacher chaired the local authority health and wellbeing committee
- Rural Primary School. Serving ex-industrial rural town with high levels of unemployment. 187 pupils. The school was regarded locally as an example 'good practice' in relation to health and wellbeing, featuring in local authority publications.

Four teachers were interviewed in each school. The selection of teachers was advised by the head teacher, on the basis of criteria outlined in the initial approach to the school. The focus of the study on the aspects of health and wellbeing seen to be the 'responsibility of all' rather than on the taught curriculum was stressed. The head teachers were asked to identify teachers who were interested in health and wellbeing in a broader sense, rather than people who taught subjects such as home economics which are seen to be key areas for delivery of the health and wellbeing curriculum. The table below, shows the pseudonyms and roles of the participating teachers.

Table showing participating teachers

Pseudonym	Role
City academy	
John	Responsibility for health and wellbeing across school
Linda	Principal Teacher of Geography
Luke	Design and technology teacher, chair of health and wellbeing group
Tina	Guidance teacher
City primary	
Belinda	P5 class teacher
Charles	P1/2 class teacher and behaviour support
Morag	Depute head teacher
Sharon	Support for learning teacher
Rural academy	
Carol	Biology teacher
Claire	Head teacher
Fiona	Guidance teacher
Graham	English teacher
Rural primary	
Barry	Depute head teacher and P6 class teacher
Kathryn	P5 teacher
Kirsten	Nursery teacher
Michaela	Head teacher

8.2 Evidence of Patterns in the Data

When discussing the data, it is important to consider whether there were patterns between the respondents that justify treating them as separate groups within the discussion. In this case the interview data came from two groups: policy actors and teachers. According to Bernstein (2000), policy actors and teachers would form two different 'speech communities', and the discourses would be subject to change as they moved between the two. In designing the study, it was anticipated that it might capture a 'genre chain' (Fairclough 2003) whereby discourses in written policy were recontextualised by the policy community, then further recontextualised by the practitioner community, giving rise to distinctive differences between the communities. It had been an expectation that the two sets of data would have distinct differences. In fact, the themes that could be seen in policy actors' data were also present in the teachers' data, and vice versa, hence there was no evidence of recontextualisation between the genres of policy actor and practitioner. There was a wide variety of discursive positions in both sets of data, but no evidence to suggest that the two sets of participants could be categorised as holding clearly divergent positions. Consequently, teachers' and policy actors' interviews are discussed together.

When Bernstein (2000) was writing, policy texts were written in hard copy and would be passed in a linear fashion between national policy makers, local policy makers and schools, with documentation being produced at each level. Dissemination was a step-like process with little shared discussion between the actors in each group. At the time of this study policy information flow was quite different as all interviewees in this study were using the 'Curriculum for Excellence' website as their main source of information, and this complex site was equally available to all users. Possibly the digitalisation of policy texts has broken down some of the barriers between speech communities.

Similarly, at practitioner level there was variety between interviewees, but no clear evidence of difference at an institutional level. There is no evidence of the schools operating as separate 'speech communities'. This aligns with Fairclough's (2010) observation that institutions are not monolithic, and that there will be a plurality of ideologies and discourses within any institution. The most noticeable pattern was the within-school variability of discourses. In each case there were four quite distinct transcripts. Equally, no clear pattern could be discerned to distinguish between the local authorities (urban and rural), or between the different school sectors (primary and secondary). In fact, the only pattern that could be noted was the absence of any pattern across the different groups! For this reason, neither the school, nor the authority nor the sector was a useful focus for analysis of the teachers' data. Hence all the interview data are reported together.

8.3 Findings from the Interviews

This section will explore how the study participants understood their role in supporting wellbeing in school. It will show how the written policy was reshaped and reformed as it moved from into the policy and practice communities. It will demonstrate how the participants adopted or adapted the discourses of the state as they recontextualised policy within the context of their own personal and professional circumstances. The section will demonstrate how, in some cases the policy discourses which framed wellbeing as a servant to learning were supported, reinforced, or further extended, whereas at the same time, and sometimes in the same interviews some teachers and policy actors drew from a different understanding of the relationship between learning and wellbeing.

Fairclough (2010) pointed out that most people are relatively unaware of the ideologies that underpin their discourses and they may not be 'committed' to them. Individuals can occupy several positions simultaneously that may in some cases be ideologically incompatible. In some cases, participants drew from different discourses disconnectedly in the same transcript. More interesting is the way that some interviewees interwove different discourses, to make their own sense of this complex field. This is most evident in the Belinda's discussion which is reported at the end of this section.

8.3.1 Naturalisation of Policy Discourses

By far the most commonly adopted discourses were those which echoed the written policy, drawing of the vocabulary of the Scottish Government policies. It was very evident that the notion that schools had a place in directing the personal lives of children, justified by the wellbeing policy had very largely been accepted as common sense.

Most frequently, psychological discourses were adopted that echoed the written policies, and were often lexicalised with similar vocabulary of the skills of self-management. For example, in the excerpt below Charles (City Primary teacher), discussed happiness and sadness in terms of the 'appropriate degree' of feeling and 'being in control of your emotions'. This is linked to social skills, articulated as forming and 'holding on' to relationships through awareness of your own behaviour.

> *I think for somebody to have wellbeing they have to* ***understand their emotions,*** *um... so... there are times when they're sad, there are times when they're happy, but to um...* ***the appropriate degree*** *because if somebody is not um... if there isn't a sense of wellbeing if the slightest thing has happened* ***they might be overly sad or overly angry*** *um... and I think being in* ***control of your emotions is one aspect of it*** *but I think there are a lot of different aspects of it. It could be about forming...* ***being able to form good relationships*** *um... with friends, with adults, and* ***holding on to those relationships***. *Um... just being aware of your own behaviour and being able to take into account you're...* ***take responsibility for your own behaviour***.

This is a sense of wellbeing as personal responsibility, being able to understand and regulate both the inner self and social behaviours in a way which is acceptable. It normalises emotions, placing boundaries around what can be acceptably expressed, or perhaps even felt, within the school setting. It ignores the external factors that may give rise to complex emotions in children. This is an example of how the dominant or discourses of policy have been naturalised in the speech of educationalists. It illustrates what Ecclestone and Hayes (2009a) describe as schools attempting to 'change the subject' through their work on emotional literacy.

Participants often also associated wellbeing with resilience; a key policy issue. To take one example, Susan (Education policy actor), described wellbeing was evident as being able to 'cope' with the harsh reality of everyday life:

> *I just think life for everyone is stressful and difficult and I think the thing about wellbeing is that* ***kind of being at one with yourself*** *and feeling... waking up in the morning and looking forward to the day ahead and* ***feeling that you can cope with it and enjoy it****, so that's why I think it's really, really important.*

Implicit in this quotation is an assumption that life for young people is difficult and they must develop skills of emotional self-management in order to handle adversity. Again, wellbeing was seen as highly individualised, with an inward facing lens self-control as the way to approach problems. This takes a pessimistic view of life, and portrays individuals as vulnerable, passive recipients of whatever life throws at them (Ecclestone 2012) Rather than taking an outward looking view, to encourage to try and engage with the causes of their difficulties, and try to make changes for the better, they are asked to look inwards to change themselves (Clack 2012).

Other responses reiterated the links made in policy between the psychological discourse and the discourse of care by identifying how the teacher's caring actions (or lack of them) affect how children feel about themselves. Here Michaela (Rural Primary, Head teacher) identifies how sensitive relationships support children emotionally:

> *I think the* ***teachers here are very very good at picking up*** *...* ***and on just the small things*** *as well so I suppose you said... I can talk about the bigger picture but the* ***teachers are much better at saying how are you?*** *And... that's the emotional literacy side of it and when we were talking about emotional literacy of children and what we could do*

Again this reiterates the policy assertion that it is through caring relationships that children will be supported to develop their social and emotional literacy. It also confirms the suggestion that ostensibly 'caring relationships' that are provided through organisations of state can aimed at shaping the behaviour and subjectivities of the recipients of care (Hendrick 2005).

8.3.2 Wellbeing as a Prerequisite of Learning

The dominant discursive link made between wellbeing and learning which repeated extensively across the transcripts was that health and wellbeing was a prerequisite for children to be able to learn. This discursive theme was present in some format in 20 of the 25 interviews, but, equally notable was its absence from five of the transcripts. In this context social and emotional wellbeing was foregrounded, with participants also invoking the themes of care, and physical health. Thus there was ample evidence of the main policy discourse being directly adopted in the practice environment.

For example, Susan (Education policy actor) portrayed this as common sense, remarking:

> *So I suppose . . . I mean it doesn't take an awful lot to work out the fact that if a young person's health is in good shape, they're going to learn better.*

In conveying this relationship as obvious, not taking 'an awful lot to work out', it can be seen that this discourse has been naturalised, and passed without question in conversation. In the same vein, Nigel (Rural Authority, quality improvement officer) invoked the psychological discursive theme saying that:

> *I think to some extent if children aren't happy and uh . . . if their needs aren't being met then they're not going to be effective learners so to some extent uh . . . I think we need to get the health and wellbeing right before you'll move on to other areas of learning.*

Whilst Gillian located her remarks in the discursive theme of physical health promotion with the statement:

> *I think if a child isn't healthy or has um . . . good wellbeing then they're not going to be able to learn you know even just little things like having breakfast in the morning, and you know they're more likely to have good concentration during the day.*

Similarly, Hilary (formerly Scottish Health Promoting Schools Unit) commented:

> *In order for children to learn they need to be emotionally, socially, and physically* ***in a place that*** *will allow them to do that*

The metaphor that conceptualised wellbeing as being 'in a place' to learn was widely used in the transcripts of policy actors and teachers. This is not an expression that is used in written policy, so this demonstrates how the concept of wellbeing as a prerequisite for learning has been re-lexicalised as it moves through the communities of education professionals.

Similarly, for example Michaela (Rural Primary, head teacher), used this phrase as she articulated her understanding of health and wellbeing:

> *Health and wellbeing is every single aspect, it's the full picture, so it's the social, it's the emotional, it's the physical, it's . . . its everything about that child. So . . . for a child to be, as I say,* ***in a place where they can learn****, all of* ***those pieces of the jigsaw need to be in place.***

Michaela's excerpt invokes another commonly used concept amongst teachers, also involving the word 'place'. She refers to wellbeing as a 'jigsaw' requiring its pieces to be 'in place'. The idea of wellbeing, or its constituent parts being put 'in place' by the work of professionals is a recontextualisation of the GIRFEC wheel, whereby deficits in the constituent parts of wellbeing are identified and remedied on a piece by piece basis, in order to support the learning of the child.

Again, we can see that the main argument for health and wellbeing as part of the school responsibility, because it serves learning has been widely and uncritically adopted in the school community. It exemplifies the ideas of Fielding's (2007) 'high performance learning community' whereby personal aspects of children's lives were supported because they were instrumental in achieving the goals of the school. In the following section, there will be examples of where this understanding is strengthened and deepened to show how wellbeing is not only a prerequisite of learning – the two have been conflated.

8.3.3 Conflating Learning with Wellbeing

Amongst some interviewees, not only was there a re-iteration of the necessity of wellbeing for successful learning, there was also a shift towards a definition of wellbeing as the state in which learning can occur. For example, Claire (Rural Academy, head teacher) volunteered her conception of health and wellbeing, again using the phrase 'in a place to learn':

> *We decided that health and wellbeing was about well . . . we came down to a very simple definition in the end which centred around all pupils were in a happy, safe and comfortable place to learn. That they were in a position to learn and uh . . . that was the basis of our health and wellbeing.*

This example of recontextualisation is no longer a matter of vocabulary – it a conceptual shift whereby health and wellbeing is not simply a support for learning, instead becomes *discursively congruent* with the capacity to learn. The very definition of wellbeing is bound up with educational success. In this view, a child who is learning well, must be in a good state of wellbeing and vice versa. This is intensifying the policy position that wellbeing is the servant of learning, to a perspective whereby wellbeing can only be judged through the 'successful learner'. In this context, a seemingly slight discursive shift in the interpretation of policy, has the effect of soundlessly extending the reach of the state, so that children's very being is judged only in the context of what the school desires for the children.

Harry (City Authority, quality improvement officer) also articulated very clearly that, health and wellbeing served the development of the Scottish policy aim of the 'four capacities' (confident individual, successful learner, effective contributor and responsible citizen). Health and wellbeing, in his view was indistinguishable from the achievement of the four capacities. The exchange below arose from a question asking how he would recognise health and wellbeing in a young person.

> *Harry cont . . . And that's what we need to keep going back to, we need to keep going back to the four capacities, that's where this (health and wellbeing policy) all lies behind . . . that's why we've changed the curriculum. That's why we're doing all this work in school because we decided right from the ..or so I believe . . . that actually the young person that we were producing at the end of their educational experience wasn't a young person who was ready to . . . always ready to take on, and take the next step. Academically they might be very strong but actually in a lot of other areas they may well have been quite wobbly.*
>
> *Interviewer: Yeah. Yes.*
>
> *Harry: I think its . . . I think you need to keep going back, health and wellbeing when you look at the four capacities it just fits perfectly doesn't it?*

So strong was Harry's belief that the four capacities *were* health and wellbeing that he suggested that if young people demonstrate the four capacities, then that was *evidence* of a good state of wellbeing:

> *If as . . . a school community in its widest sense can produce young people that have achieved the four capacities within the Curriculum for Excellence, then I would suggest then that we are . . . producing young people who have a good knowledge of health and wellbeing and who have the . . . variety of skills to have reasonable health and wellbeing themselves.*

In this conceptualisation, not only does health and wellbeing support the development of the four capacities, it has *morphed into* the four capacities. In this elision of concepts, the policy rhetoric is recontexualised in a way that further entrenches its ideology. In these sentences the personal wellbeing of children has become conflated with the governmental view of the 'good' citizen. In Fielding's (2007) terms this is the way the 'high performance learning organisation would operate in its 'totalitarian mode' where 'the personal and the functional collapse into each other'. The wellbeing of children has been discursively appropriated by the agenda of character development.

This example demonstrates how public servants, who have devoted their lives to the education and care of children can, inadvertently support capitalist agendas (Apple 2006). Arguably, the acceptance of psychological health and wellbeing as a tool for learning and its further conflation with both learning capacity and with the four capacities, demonstrates how discourses operate 'behind the back of the subject' in a context where 'rules of the game' are opaque to participants (Wodak and Meyer 2009). As these concepts became naturalised in the discourses of teachers, they were accepted as consensus (van Dijk 1997). Shrouded in the kindly terminology of wellbeing, the neoliberal ideology underpinning the discourse was not visible to the teachers. In all likelihood the teachers were unaware that actions which they believe to be undertaken in the spirit of caring for children are unwittingly contributing to the competitive human capital project.

8.3.4 Health and Wellbeing as a Solution to Other Problems

Connected with the conceptualisation of wellbeing as being 'in a place to learn' is the opposite association, that children who are not learning must be lacking in health and wellbeing. Consequently, the solution to problems was often construed as working with the children to improve their sense of emotional wellbeing, which in turn, it was suggested would resolve the difficulty in learning. Across the interview transcripts were numerous examples of health and wellbeing represented as a solution to difficulties in learning, as well as behavioural problems.

For Michaela, (Rural Primary, head teacher) the use of her health and wellbeing initiative was viewed as a vehicle to address what she saw as a whole school malaise. She described how, on taking over her school she had been dissatisfied with the level of motivation amongst the children to engage with their learning, and how her response had been to introduce a health and wellbeing programme:

> *There was a feeling when I came into the school that there needed to be – very difficult to explain – there needed to be another level of energy to the school. The children needed to be motivated, they needed to be in a good place to behave and be interested in learning.*
>
> *. . . . . . I think it was a case of OK well* ***if we have children in the right place to learn*** *and* ***we do that through a health and wellbeing programme of work*** *and also we have interesting contexts for them to learn then the 2 go hand in hand with increased attainment, achievement and perhaps an increase in behaviour and good . . . the positive behaviours rather than the negative behaviours so that's where I came from.*

Michaela's comments demonstrated the complex ways in which health and wellbeing, learning, attainment, achievement and behaviour are seen to interlink, but notably the underlying solution to problems in other areas was to focus on health and wellbeing. At another point she referred to health and wellbeing as the 'crutch to the rest of the curriculum'. Thus wellbeing was not discursively construed as the outcome of high quality learning; rather wellbeing was seen to underpin success in the other areas.

Across the interviews health and wellbeing was something of a panacea in addressing difficulties of various sorts that emerged in a school setting. Sharon (City Primary teacher) gave sessions in 'understanding anger' so that children who arrived upset by events at home could be settled into 'a good place to learn'. Similarly, Charles (City Primary teacher), in discussing how social issues can be detrimental to learning, described how he taught social skills to children in the hope of better classroom behaviour and learning for themselves and their classmates.

Not only was a school focus on health and wellbeing presented by interviewees as a solution to problems with behaviour, motivation and learning, it was sometimes construed as a compensation for deficits in other aspects of children's lives, in particular poor parenting, linked to deprivation. A governmental steer on the notion of school-based health and wellbeing interventions as a solution to the problems encountered within the family was provided by Stephen (Scottish Government):

> *I think my interpretation of it is also that um . . . the health and wellbeing of the individual learner is something that facilitates their ability to learn so . . . if you have somebody . . . if you have a child coming from a very chaotic background and their ability to learn is probably compromised to some extent by that environmental factor and so . . . the schools or other institution where learning takes place . . . their ability to if you like bring some order to that person concerned about their experience and life will in itself facilitate their ability to learn more effectively.*

Whilst the problem articulated here, clearly lies in the environment, the response to the difficulties in learning is a school-based attempt to work on the child's wellbeing. Social or societal problems are addressed by seeking to bring about changes in children.

In identifying psychological health and wellbeing as a kind of remedy to a number of educational dilemmas, including low motivation, poor behaviour and lack of progress in learning, the interviewees also echoed policy in construing improved childhood wellbeing as a solution to problems that may be caused by wider societal issues. However, in places this notion was individualised more directly than was the written policy. Whereas GIRFEC (Scottish Government 2012) was always careful to construe poor health and wellbeing as a deficiency in the *care* of the child, some interviewees recontextualised the problem as a deficit in the child. Then the solution was viewed as working on the child to develop such skills as coping, resilience, anger management, social skills and so on. Rather than addressing the problem, the child was being taught how to cope with it, or perhaps in spite of it.

To some extent this can be seen as a contemporary twist on a well-established approach. Whilst the children are not construed as 'bad' or demonised as they may have been in the past (Coppock 2005), they are nonetheless the site of correction of a problem whose origins lie elsewhere. The use of the benign language of health and wellbeing allows these corrective strategies to be delivered under the guise of 'support' or 'care', whilst fundamentally still finding the fault to be in the child, with the professional response aimed at bringing about change in the child, as described by Hendrick (2005). In this way 'wellbeing' provides a discursive tool for socialising children in ways that are helpful to schools.

8.3.5 Tensions Between Learning and Health and Wellbeing

Amongst policy actors there was a view that of the three areas in 'Curriculum for Excellence' that were the cross-curricular 'responsibility of all', (i.e. literacy, numeracy and health and wellbeing), the most poorly resourced was health and wellbeing, giving rise to a suggestion that it was marginalised by the more academic aspects of the curriculum. Both local authority quality improvement officers expressed a sense that over-ardent pursuit of high standards in literacy and numeracy was detrimental to their attempts to embed good practices of health and wellbeing in schools. Hence Nigel (Rural Authority, quality improvement officer) suggested that in the competition with literacy and numeracy that wellbeing is a 'poor country cousin'. In particular, in secondary schools, developments in health and wellbeing had recently been side-lined by the introduction of a new examination system. What is very clear from these accounts is that health and wellbeing was viewed by these participants as separate from academic learning, particularly literacy and numeracy. There is no sense that literacy and numeracy might contribute to wellbeing.

A small number of teachers also identified a tension between learning and health and wellbeing, suggesting that one somehow impeded the development of the other. Charles (City primary teacher) used the term 'fighting balance' to describe the relationship between attainment (in literacy and numeracy) and a positive experience of health and wellbeing, suggesting that he felt he had to minimise his focus on health and wellbeing in order to address academic attainment. Charles did not conceptualise development literacy and numeracy as essential aspects of wellbeing, nor did he view the experience of learning as helpful to wellbeing. Instead he saw time spent on them as interfering with other work that he would like to do to support emotional development.

In a secondary school context, Tina (City Academy, teacher) also identified antagonism between learning and wellbeing, in the way in which learning was sometimes approached in secondary schools. She cited examination pressure as a stressful product of contemporary schooling that could be damaging to the emotional wellbeing of her pupils. For Tina, it wasn't learning *per se* that was potentially undermining of pupils' health and wellbeing, but, she identified aspects of the way education is organised as potentially very stressful. Ironically, in her Guidance role she invoked the discursive theme of care to counteract the influences of schooling.

Another way in which the policy was recontextualised in the interviews was the reinforcement of the silos into which learning and health and wellbeing seem to fall. In 'Curriculum for Excellence' literacy, numeracy and health and wellbeing are seen as the three cross-curricular areas that should be incorporated 'across learning', i.e. seen as a consideration in any lesson. In some cases, interview participants echoed the structure of 'Curriculum for Excellence' in the way that they represented literacy, numeracy and health and wellbeing in the same three silos that they appear in print, whilst also seeing them in tension with each other. Policy actors pointed to different funding streams for the three areas of literacy, numeracy and health and wellbeing which have resulted in a disconnect between them. The teachers conceptualised wellbeing as something different and apart from learning; in competition with learning, rather than integrally connected. The fragmented format of 'Curriculum for Excellence', coupled with financial constraints has resulted in a discursive dislocation of health and wellbeing from aspects of learning that are fundamental to the opportunities children and young people have to lead a life of value both now and in the future. Although this featured in a minority of transcripts, it none the less makes the interesting point that both at policy level and in schools there was some perception that health and wellbeing competed with the literacy and numeracy, both for time and for resources. Instead of seeing the development of literacy and numeracy as integral to and essential for wellbeing, these interviewees represented time spent in these curricular areas as detracting from time that could be devoted to health and wellbeing. We can see how the compartmentalisation of the written policy has been transferred directly to the way that these interviewees constructed their 'mental map' (van Dijk 2006a) of the relationship between learning and wellbeing. The notion of flourishing through curricular learning seemed to missing.

8.3.6 Alternatives to Policy Discourses- Wellbeing as Flourishing

It was apparent from the interviews that some participants recontextualised the policy in ways that drew from a wider understanding of wellbeing. As predicted by Bernstein (2000) the 'discursive gap' between policy text and the practice community provided a space where individuals could bring their own values, experiences and understandings to bear as they interpreted and translated the policy for their own context (Singh et al. 2013). In these examples the policies were not passively received by a community of 'empty vessels', but were instead actively incorporated into an existing mental map (van Dijk 2006a), which included some fundamental understandings of what, to them, was involved in being a teacher.

In some cases, interview respondents spoke in general terms of wellbeing as 'happiness'. For example, Kirsten (Rural Primary, nursery teacher) said,

> *I think wellbeing is ... um ... the first thing I would look for is a happy child, a child that smiles.*

Although this seems perhaps to be the most obvious association that anybody might make with wellbeing, it does not resonate very closely with policy. Educational policy steers away from naming emotions such as happiness, or manifestations such as smiling, favouring instead psychological attributes such as confidence, or self-efficacy. This is simple example of how policy was recontextualised by some teachers, who, in this case drew from everyday experiences of children's emotions to and used a more day-to-day language to frame their own interpretations of childhood wellbeing.

Similarly, Linda (City Academy, principal teacher of geography), drew from a different lexicon when she volunteered her conceptualisation of wellbeing.

> *Um ... I think here we'd like to see our kids* ***thriving*** *in* ***whatever they're doing*** *and* ***actively involved*** *within the school.*

In using the word 'thriving' Linda came the closest of any interviewee to a word synonymous with 'flourishing', conceptualised as leading a life you have reason to value, following Sen (e.g. 2009). Implicit in this definition is the concept of wellbeing as how a life is lived rather than simply how a person feels, and therefore places a value on opportunities for children to do things that they find interesting, worthwhile or enjoyable. For Linda thriving involved taking an active role within the life of the school, developing good relationships which in turn afforded opportunities for children to express their interests and be supported in exploring them.

The discourse of flourishing was prominent in a minority of transcripts. These sources provided a rich source of data whose ideology and vocabulary were not solely sourced from contemporary policies of wellbeing. However, the discourse of flourishing did not sit alone in the transcripts – there was no simple dichotomy between those who talked of flourishing and those who did not. Most interviewees drew from a range of different discourses and these overlapped within their conversations as shown below.

Morag (City Primary, depute head) articulated her understanding of childhood wellbeing by describing a group of children enjoying a trip from their inner city school to visit a partner school located in the countryside.

> *It's in the middle of nowhere um ...* ***the children were just enthralled*** *being out in the country,* ***all the different smells, all the different sights****, and animals and what have you*

The excerpt above provides a vision of wellbeing achieved through the stimulation of experiencing a, largely unfamiliar, outdoor environment, describing the children as being 'enthralled'. Again, wellbeing is associated with the things that children do, and the experiences that they have. Interestingly, this excerpt also supports the arguments that are made that close connections with nature are supportive of wellbeing, and is one of the few examples in this project that demonstrated the emerging discourse of sustainability.

The definition of wellbeing as 'leading a life you have reason to value' is also predicated on individuals understanding what is of value, and is based on an assumption of diversity between people. Within the concept of 'flourishing' is an idea that children should have opportunities to understand and develop their unique characters, and to follow their interests, articulated by Biesta (2010) as 'subjectification' This was articulated clearly by John (City Academy, teacher), whose interview focussed on the provision of a wide array of extracurricular opportunities. When asked how he conceptualised health and wellbeing, he gave an unequivocal response:

> *I think it's very simple,* ***I think it's about having a sense of yourself, you know knowing who you are****, um . . . what makes up who you are,*

As will be discussed later, John's approach to his work was very much driven by his desire to help children to better understand the opportunities available to them.

The theme of autonomy was further developed by Barry (Rural Primary, deputy head teacher and class teacher), who saw wellbeing as engaging actively with the world. In particular he focussed on supporting children to pursue matters of importance to them in order to be in a position to achieve those things that they valued. Where children encountered obstacles to their plans, he encouraged them to tackle the difficulties, urging them to look outward to bring about changes, rather than looking inward for resources to cope with the problems.

Furthermore, Barry represented this notion of flourishing through active engagement as linked to the discursive theme of care, by saying:

> *. . . . . . But that's only developed in the school by you continually doing it as the ethos within the school, the ethos of the school has got to be supportive.*

Like Linda, he was suggesting that supportive relationships within the school foster conditions in which children can develop autonomy.

8.3.7 Learning for Flourishing

Those participants who conceptualised wellbeing in the philosophical sense of flourishing, also identified the vital role for teaching and learning in enabling children to be able to lead lives that they had reason to value both in the present and in the future. This perspective saw an intrinsic value of education for the wellbeing of the child, and identified teaching and learning as the key contribution that teachers, uniquely amongst professionals, could make to children's wellbeing. Although representations of the discursive strand of learning *for* flourishing were in the minority in this data, they are highly significant to this study, and therefore are reported in some detail.

Broadly speaking, the data focussed on two (overlapping) topics, firstly the impact of the *experience* of learning on wellbeing and secondly the impact of the *curricular content* on learning. These have implications for the pedagogical approaches adopted by teachers and for the choices made about what should be taught. Both of these were construed in different contexts as supporting childhood flourishing. These will be considered in turn.

John, (City Academy, teacher) was a strong advocate of experiential learning for wellbeing. As the co-ordinator of the school's health and wellbeing committee, he oversaw a comprehensive array of extra-curricular activities, including music, sport, foreign travel, apprenticeships at the local radio station, links to the territorial army, visits to the local library, membership of local clubs and associations and much more. For John, wellbeing was about expanding opportunities to do different things. In the following passage he gave more detail of a specific example – a school trip to the Ardeche in France – in which he sets out to introduce the children to as wide a range of novel activities as possible:

> *We're actually going to spend a week there the next time. Um... but these kids a lot of them have never... they've never applied for a passport, they've never been out of Scotland perhaps, never been on a ferry, we even set up experiences... we do get uh... escargot and frogs legs, and they eat them you know? Good on them!* ***It's about making the world a... bigger view isn't it?***

John articulated an understanding of the concept of wellbeing as having a sense of yourself. To him, the reason for offering all these activities was to help young people to develop an understanding of themselves and their place in the world:

> *Why do we do this and why do we do that? It's not just to give the kids a good time, there has to be obviously... um... an intention and the* ***intention is always about improving their knowledge of themselves*** *and also you know?*

Here we see a discourse that frames learning as a broad set of experiences which link to the humanist notion of 'unfolding' of the unique individual (Kickbusch et al. 2012), framed within the context of engaging with the wider society.

John's account of health and wellbeing was unique in the interview sample as it focused entirely on extra-curricular activities. John saw few links between his work and the formal curriculum, suggesting simply that the extracurricular health and wellbeing efforts of the staff rendered schooling more palatable. Perhaps, in this way he also contributed to the view that curricular learning was oppositional to wellbeing.

However, other transcripts identified the experience of learning through the formal curriculum as important to health and wellbeing, and in this context pedagogy was considered. This was highlighted particularly in the transcripts of Belinda and Barry, whose accounts of their work offered some practical detail. For Belinda (City Primary, teacher) wellbeing in the classroom was entirely congruent with a learning experience that was participatory, that provided children with opportunities to take ownership and to engage actively in the *process* of learning. Belinda's account of wellbeing linked very closely to the 'Curriculum for Excellence' approach to learning more generally. However, whilst the policy documentation falls short of making explicit linkages between the preferred pedagogies and the health and wellbeing strategies, Belinda had made these links for herself. The following short excerpt offers a concise summary of Belinda's overall position:

> *It's (wellbeing is) all about* ***making the learning appropriate and valid and meaningful to the children*** *in the situation and the context that they find themselves in,* ***and helping them to be able to transfer those skills from one situation to another****. And that surely must make them feel healthy inside and out.*

Generally, literature on wellbeing in schools says little about the impact of pedagogy on wellbeing. However, an Australian study that sought the views of over 600 school students (age 6–17) reported that children and young people identified creative and supportive pedagogies as relevant to their wellbeing (Simmons et al. 2015). Belinda's approach demonstrates an understanding of how her pedagogical choices can impact on the children's sense of worth and value in their education.

For Barry (Rural Primary, depute head and P7 teacher), health and wellbeing was closely associated with agency, or having some control over shaping one's life. This is very much in keeping with the Capability Approach, in which having the agency and autonomy to pursue that things that are of value, is a key element of wellbeing (Sen 2009). Barry saw his role in supporting wellbeing as adopting approaches to teaching and learning that fostered independence, and problem solving. He was particularly keen that children should learn not to passively accept situations that they were unhappy with. He sought to provide learning opportunities for children to be proactive, fostering what he called a 'can do' attitude. He located his approach in collaborative, shared working between the children:

> *I think its [wellbeing is] people being in a position where* ***they feel that they have a larger control over what happens to them****, … But it's giving them the tools and the ammunition as to how to do it. Alright that's not going to work who else could I contact? …… Its giving them the strategies that there's not just one way of doing something there are various ways. But* ***it's getting their minds to work in such a way that they can think out strategies and actions*** *for themselves.*

Barry illustrated his conception of wellbeing with frequent references to a forthcoming school trip, for which the children were involved in all aspects of planning, organising and fundraising. This included negotiating with the local community in order to raise sufficient funds. Children were involved in face to face visits to local business people, and in writing to the local (celebrity) landowner, requesting support. This, Barry linked to the formal literacy curriculum, saying:

> *I mean yeah they were practicing letter writing, they were practicing…all the language…they were doing these things but not in a meaningless way.*

Thus, for him opportunities to support wellbeing (as agency) could be found by taking a creative approach to meeting the formal demands of the curriculum.

The importance of curricular content for health and wellbeing was raised by one policy actor, Margaret (Education Scotland). Her understanding of wellbeing related strongly to a concept of empathy for other people, and she spoke about how this could be addressed within the formal curriculum. She put a strong focus, on learning about other cultures:

> *that's not just about individual... it's not just about a view of society that you know my mental health, it's about* ***collective responsibility*** *and looking at you know wider issues, it might be looking at children....* ***international education.*** *I've seen some really super work about well... it's about children from different cultures and a link between schools but actually when you unpick that although* ***they're learning about the cultures*** *and they're doing various things about fund raising and whatever,* ***they're actually learning about empathy, you know without someone saying we're going to do a lesson on empathy today.***

This is a view of the purpose of education which aligns with the philosophical stance, of education serving to support the individual to live well within the world. This resonates with a point made by Suissa (2008), that the best way for children to understand their emotions is through the curriculum. She suggests that there are ample opportunities within the existing curricular arrangements for children to learn about their emotions by studying the actions and the expressions of others. Margaret later emphasised this point by saying:

> *How can you do World War II without looking at issues of you know persecution and human relationships and kind of man's inhumanity to man?*

In another example of the curriculum supporting wellbeing, Graham, (Rural Academy, principal teacher of English) described how, in his view, literacy was key to self-expression and understanding the views of others. In the following extract he comments on the value of reading literature to understanding important themes in human lives:

> *The themes that we deal with as well um... like, death, love, friendship you know the biggies that we all experience, the universal themes, um... seeing characters in books or short stories or poems deal with these kinds of things allows them a kind of detachment to examine reactions.*

In this excerpt we can see the study of literature as a means to understanding a range of experiences and emotions. This differs from discourses focusing on self-scrutiny and self-management. Instead it provides an example of curricular learning supporting the emotional development of young people through examining powerful experiences of others.

Moreover, Graham identified how the expressive aspect of his English classes also contributed to the wellbeing of his pupils as enhanced literacy enabled them to explore and express their own feelings.

> *Showing the children how to actually express themselves um... through writing whether it's a diary or reflective writing or a poem can be really really beneficial because it gives them an extra outlet for all these things that they're going through it's (teenage years) a really tough time in our lives and I think we all recognise that.*

Creativity, more generally has been is understood by writers as being interwoven with human flourishing. For example, Gordon and O'Toole (2015) suggest that creativity lies 'at the very heart of what it means for children to lead happy, healthy and meaningful lives in which they feel recognised for who they are and feel belonging and a sense of agency to express themselves' (p345).

The perspectives offered by the participants reported in this section have resonated with Fielding's (2007) notion of the person-centred learning community, in which education is only justifiable in terms of enriching the lives of young people and supporting them to better understand themselves in relation to others. In this model the functional aspects of schooling serve to enhance the personal aspects of children's lives. Like John Macmurray's (2012) call that education should be aimed at 'learning to be human' or Nussbaum's (2010) demands that learning should enrich the 'soul', we can see that these teachers were, each in their own way seeking to do that. Their discursive understanding of the 'wellbeing agenda' was articulated in support of this view of education.

Their perspectives also illustrate something of the way that discourse works. Clearly, there is not one single policy discourse that changes instantly when governments introduce new agendas. In reality, there are multiple discourses operating in the educational world simultaneously, emanating from current and previous policies forming a rich and complex 'policy archive' (Ball et al. 2012) which educators may draw from in order to build their views of the world. On top of this teachers and others bring their own histories to bear on creating their view of the world (Grue 2009) and may draw from wider ethical, moral, political and academic frameworks to form their understanding of who they are as professionals and what they are trying the achieve. In these examples the interviewees were not passively ascribing to discourses that acted behind their back, they were active in their assessment and evaluation of their own discursive positions.

To finish this section, I will return to Belinda (City Primary P5 teacher), who adeptly interwove a discourse of flourishing (through meaningful pedagogy) with a discourse of care. To her, wellbeing involved provision of meaningful learning experiences, but within that she articulated issues of classroom relationships and individual feelings, as shown below:

> *Now what I do is especially in the likes of a science and project work* ***I ask the children,*** *we'll look at a topic and I say* ***what sort of things are you interested in?*** *And I always explain to them it's* ***pointless me planning a topic of work for you if you've done it already or you're not interested.*** *I say because it's your learning that will be affected. So they're actually very happy to come out with an idea of telling me what they've learnt already, what they already know, so we can sort of do a little recap on that but then build on their interests.*
>
> ***And I also like to ask them how they think they're going to learn these things and how they're going to share it.*** *So it's not just about sitting down, being taught, remembering. It's a bit more about sitting down,* ***agreeing on what's going to be taught, agreeing on the ways that are going to be used to teach, and then going and sharing what you've found out.*** *And that's really interesting the sharing part because that is* ***encouraging, making children feel that they are important,*** *that what they know is important and it's important enough to go and share.*

Firstly, she used the discursive theme of flourishing by considering the meaningfulness of the learning experience for the children, and avoiding, activities which the children might view as 'pointless'. Hence she seeks to ensure the students are involved in activities that they have reason to value in the present. She addressed issues of relationships and ethos by locating the learning communally, talking about 'agreeing' on activities and 'sharing' what has been learnt. This resonates with Nodding's (2012) notion of 'true' care based on a dialogic relationship. It also demonstrates the 'joy' of learning, though shared pedagogic endeavour between teachers and pupils, a process that Griffiths (2012) refers to as both eudaimonic and socially just.

Finally, she draws on the psychological discourse of health and wellbeing by suggesting that this makes the children 'feel that they are important.' Belinda's transcript demonstrates how the different discourses of wellbeing, whilst they have emerged from different academic stables can be interwoven in the pedagogies of teachers. For Belinda, the caring relationship is not conceptualised as creating an environment to enhance emotional control in order to better engage with learning. Instead the caring environment is a fundamental part, and consequence of the pedagogical approach, which in turn allows the children to flourish.

8.4 Summary

This chapter has explored how the discourses of wellbeing articulated in policy are recontextualised by teachers and policy actors. It shows how much of the interview data echoed written policy by fore-grounding wellbeing as an individualised state of emotional and social literacy, linked to a sense of physical wellbeing, and supported by a caring environment. Like the policy, wellbeing was largely construed as a pre-requisite of learning.

To some extent the policy position had been further entrenched by a conflation between a state of wellbeing and the capacity learn. This was sometimes captured in the expression that conceptualised wellbeing as 'in a good place to learn'. Moreover, in one instance a participant offered a definition of wellbeing that was congruent with Scotland's 'four capacities', which are the governmental view of a 'good citizen. Thus the understanding of wellbeing had been merged conceptually with the contemporary vision of a model pupil. Following from that assumption, poor school performance or behaviour was sometimes portrayed indication of a poor sense of wellbeing, which could be remedied by offering appropriate individualised support in developing the emotional 'skills' of anger-management, resilience and so on. In these instances, 'within child' solutions were sought to problems that may have their roots elsewhere.

The data also show that in some cases policy had been recontexualised in ways which drew from wider experience or values of the participants. In these cases, teachers saw their role as educators as being the main contribution that they made to wellbeing. Wellbeing was seen to be an outcome of a positive experience of schooling. These teachers adopted a discourse of flourishing as both the process of learning and the outcome of learning were seen to be a valuable contribution to children leading a life they have reason the value.

The interview transcripts also demonstrated how complex this topic is as different discourses were often sitting side by side in the same transcript, sometimes deeply interwoven in the same sentences and paragraphs. This was most clearly articulated by the primary school teacher, Belinda, who described how for her, the participatory pedagogical approach that she adopted served to ensure that learning was meaningful, so children would flourish through their learning. At the same time, she identified how the act of meaningful teaching and learning would foster good relationships, that would enhance the feelings of emotional security. It is perhaps no surprise that the discourses link together in intricate ways, but it is important to be aware of how they are knitted together, and what purposes these constructs serve.

Chapter 9
Towards a More Comprehensive Understanding of Wellbeing and Equity in Education

The discourse of wellbeing is a medium through which those in power can extend their reach into the private lives of children and families, influencing the most personal aspects of children's lives. Due to its universally positive connotations, policy changes can be ushered in, unchallenged, under the mantle of wellbeing. Powerful actions can be exerted through the use of soft vocabulary. In the context of schooling the same language can be used to describe actions which support the neo-liberal human capital project, and actions which promote human flourishing through shared educational endeavour. Both can exist side by side in the same setting. As Fielding (2011 p. 55) remarked:

> *It is not always clear which frame is dominant, whose purposes are being served, whether we are the victims of those whose interests are quite other than those we would applaud, or whether we are part of something which is likely to turn out to be fulfilling and worthy of our support.*

J. Spratt, *Wellbeing, Equity and Education*, Inclusive Learning and Educational Equity 1, DOI 10.1007/978-3-319-50066-9_9

Just as the purpose of education may be confused and contested, so the attendant discourses of wellbeing be differently invoked. The ambiguity of this situation is particularly evident in Scotland where the over-arching aims of education, the 'four capacities', (successful learner, confident individual, effective contributor and responsible citizen) have both been interpreted as descriptors of human capital (Lingard 2008), and as a means of broadening education away from pre-determined outcomes to more child-centred approaches (Priestley 2010).

This book has sought to bring some criticality to this situation, unravelling some of the, seemingly haphazard, discursive complexity, to better understand what can happen in the name of wellbeing. By identifying different understandings of wellbeing, and revealing how these may be invoked in policy, the study has unmasked the political and ideological aims that can be supported by these discourses. As educators struggle over the meaning and purpose of schooling, discourses of wellbeing are mobilised in support of different agendas. This has revealed both dangers and opportunities for equality in education.

In this final chapter, I will discuss the implications of this study in two ways. Firstly, I will synthesise the arguments developed throughout the book to demonstrate the potential hazards for social justice inherent in an uncritical naturalisation of the dominant discourse of wellbeing as operationalised skills of social and emotional literacy. Secondly, and more positively, using the Capability Approach as a framework, I will argue for a more comprehensive understanding of wellbeing and suggest a way of understanding the contribution of schools to wellbeing by bringing together all of the discourses of wellbeing in a way that enhances the freedoms of children and future adults.

9.1 Problematizing Wellbeing Discourses in Schools

The introduction of wellbeing into school policy has been dominated by a conception of an individualised set of physical, social and emotional skills and responsibilities that children are expected to enact or internalise. This approach carries assumptions of 'one size fits all' as it portrays one correct way of feeling and being, ignoring the individual, cultural and experiential differences between children, taking no account of how children themselves might understand their wellbeing (Watson et al. 2012) It is a strongly socialising agenda seeking to shape children's subjectivities in pre-determined ways. In encouraging some emotional states over others, it may actually inhibit children's freedoms to communicate some of their feelings as they understand that these are not the emotions they should be manifesting. In this way the operationalised approach to wellbeing can be seen as a coercive agenda, in which a caring vocabulary is used to normalise (Hendrick 2005), directing development towards a state sanctioned way of being.

As a part of the individualised approach, schools are invited to work with children in order to 'remedy' feelings that may be seen as negative. This decontextualizes problems, and in locating the difficulty and the solution in the child, it deflects attention from the structural or social circumstances that may give rise the problem in the first place. Thus, it has been argued that the wellbeing agenda can de-politicise childhood (Morrow and Mayall 2009), as issues such as poverty are ignored, in favour of programmes to boost resilience. Alternatively, it could be argued childhood has become the focus of political attention (Coppock 2010) and that the shift of gaze from the structural to the individual is in itself a political act. If interventions such as resilience training are construed as a solution to the intergenerational cycles of poverty and social exclusion (Ecclestone and Hayes 2009b) then the ostensibly benevolent agenda of wellbeing has a deeply political purpose.

This can be seen as an example of ‘therapeutic turn’ (Furedi 2004) in education, whereby professionals are charged with directing the emotional lives of children in an attempt by the state to manipulate the population into the type of citizen that would be most productive. The role of policy in advocating this version of wellbeing resonates with the observation of Rose (1999) who talks of governing through the ‘science of the soul’. The school based intervention in health and wellbeing can be construed as a ‘technology’ in the governance of subjectivity, aiming to enable the ‘self’ to navigate through the individualised pathways and meet the socio-political obligations of contemporary society.

I argued in Chap. 5 that the appearance of discourses of physical, social and emotional wellbeing in schools represented a migration of discourses from other professional and academic stables into education policy. As teachers are recruited to the therapeutic project and called on to pay more attention to the emotions of children, contemporary discussions of wellbeing in schools very often overlook the contribution that education itself can make to wellbeing. By ignoring the philosophical discourses of flourishing, which would view wellbeing as a life well lived then issues of the content and pedagogy are seen as separate from the discussions of wellbeing (Clack 2012). Yet this does not mean that education and wellbeing are unconnected as the psychological discourse of wellbeing can be marshalled in support of an individualised model of education.

In examining Scottish policies, it was clear that wellbeing justified its place in education policy by recurrent assertions that it served other purposes of the school. Repeatedly, though statements such as ‘health and wellbeing is a prerequisite of learning’ it was evident that a key purpose of shaping children’s subjectivities towards the well-controlled, confident, resilient individual, wellbeing was seen as a servant to other objectives of schooling, rather than an end in itself. ‘Learning’ was not confined to curricular knowledge and skills, but was seen in a broader sense as building attitudes, dispositions and character. As identified by Ecclestone (2012) the robust aspects of wellbeing such as emotional regulation and resilience were linked to ‘positive’ dispositions and, in the Scottish context to the ‘four capacities’ of ‘confident individual’, ‘successful learner’, ‘effective contributor’ and ‘responsible citizen’. Not only can the discourse of wellbeing normalise how children feel, it seems it contributes to who they actually are.

This reading of discourses of wellbeing in the school context resonates closely with Fielding's (2007) notion of the 'high performance learning organisation', which instrumentally develops an ethos of 'care' in so far as it supports the school in meeting its own operational targets. Government sponsored policies of wellbeing are carefully attuned to the economic demands for young people demonstrating the educational success and personality traits associated with high yield human capital. Arguably, through a soft sounding discourse of wellbeing the state has noiselessly invaded the subjectivities of children to shape their development in line with the demands of the neo-liberal marketplace. Interview data reported in Chap. 8 showed how, in recontextualising policy some participants had elided the concept of wellbeing with other goals, by defining wellbeing as 'in a good place to learn', or in one case as seeing it a synonymous with the 'four capacities. In the discursive gap between written policy and practice, in these examples wellbeing collapsed into the other goals of the school, or, in Fielding's (ibid) terms the personal was subsumed by the functional.

This scenario where the discourse of wellbeing is utilised by the human capital project, invites a Foucauldian interpretation. The gaze of the panopticon is focussed through the discourse of wellbeing, fostering self-surveillance, creating not only docile bodies but compliant emotions and personalities (Foucault 1977). As networks of bureaucrats and professionals exercise their bio-power locally through the kindly acts of advice and support, wellbeing is used as a tool of regulatory control as the macro-economic machine is served (Foucault 1979). The discourses of wellbeing act behind the backs of the subjects to deliver an outcome they may not have intended.

The account above where the discourse of wellbeing is used as a cover for a manipulative form of schooling where equality is seen in terms of access to the workplace and is delivered by shaping the subjectivities of children, is an all too a realistic account of what can happen if the dominant model of social and emotional literacy is accepted without examination and critique, particularly if the educational environment is solely focussed on narrow attainments. It offers a warning of what could, and probably does happen in the name of wellbeing. However, this is not the only possible interpretation of the role of wellbeing in schools, and the following section turns to the Capability approach to show how a broader understanding of discourses of wellbeing could inform and enhance a more socially democratic model of schooling.

9.2 Wellbeing, Equity and Education – Towards a More Comprehensive Understanding Through the Capability Approach

The Capability Approach starts from a position that human beings are intrinsically very diverse, and therefore any evaluation of equality must value difference. Rather than seeking to shape people in a pre-determined way, the Capability Approach raises questions about how to enable people to do the things to which they attach value. Following Sen (2009), wellbeing, conceptualised as flourishing, can be defined as 'leading a life you have reason to value', and is seen very much in terms of what people can be and do, rather than subjective accounts of how they feel. However, the format of the life and the things that are of value are not defined. Equality is conceptualised in terms of the freedoms (or capabilities) that a person has to pursue a valuable life. Education clearly has multiple roles in supporting a life of value, through the opportunities that it provides to develop the sort of valuable functionings that create freedoms for people to do and be whatever they choose. Whilst the Capability Approach acknowledges that meaningful employment can be one aspect of a valuable life, and that money can be a very useful tool for enhancing freedoms, it rejects analyses that see the purpose of human life as entirely economic. Equally it would see the purposes of education as much wider than preparation for employment.

The purpose of schooling, then, for the Capability Approach, is to enhance the freedoms that children have to achieve wellbeing, as flourishing, both in the present and in the future. Thus children develop their capabilities through the functionings that they develop at school. For example, literacy can be seen as a functioning achieved through education which opens the door to a multiplicity of valuable opportunities, and conversely a life without literacy is severely curtailed in its choices. Illiteracy can be seen as an 'unfreedom'. However, in order to develop the freedoms that can be achieved through education, children must have the freedom to access education in the first place. In this vein Gale and Molla (2015) distinguish between the capability *for* and capability *in* education. The freedoms that may affect whether children can take advantage of education include their attendance at school, safety at school, and access to the curriculum through appropriate pedagogies (Brighouse and Unterhalter 2010). This dualism is described by Wood and Deprez (2012 p.476).

> *We recognise that our professional responsibility is two-pronged: we must ensure that students can fully participate in learning experiences, and also they have opportunities to discern what they need to instantiate beings and doings they value*

Amongst the factors that will affect whether and how a child participates in learning experiences is their state of emotional and physical wellbeing.

Hence wellbeing can be seen to enhance freedoms in education at two levels. Physical and emotional wellbeing can be seen as functionings that enhance children's capabilities to engage in education, and education in turn develops further functionings that enhance freedoms to flourish through a well lived life. Sen notes that people differ in their capacity convert opportunities into valuable functionings for a multiplicity of reasons. The capacity to convert an opportunity to a functioning is termed a 'conversion factor'. Poor physical health such as hunger or illness can curtail a child's capacity to convert their school experiences into functionings, and similarly poor mental or emotional wellbeing can inhibit children's engagement with the life and learning of the school. These can both be seen as important conversion factors. Thus there is a strong argument that schools and teachers should take account of the physical and emotional wellbeing of their children and play their role in promoting and supporting good health and remediating problems. However, this is not a call for an approach that normalises emotions, (since the Capability Approach is a response to diversity, not a drive to similarity), but rather is an acknowledgement of the role that teachers have in responding to children as human beings, recognising where poor physical and emotional wellbeing may impede learning and responding with an appropriate level of care and pedagogical sensitivity.

Pedagogical approaches should be designed to expect and account for diversity between children, and seek to avoid categorisations that mark some children out as 'different' (Florian and Black-Hawkins 2011). By designing teaching and learning experiences that consider the range of individuality, whilst planning to include everybody, teachers can take account of difference through inclusive pedagogy (Spratt and Florian 2015) Based on a socio-cultural understanding of learning teachers should take into account affective aspects as they plan teaching and learning for all (Hart et al. 2004). In this sense the teaching for Capability is ethically individualistic as it pays attention to the emotional wellbeing of each and every child, but by delivering that through a community of learners it avoids the isolation of ontological individualism (Robeyns 2005). Learning in this way simultaneously serves individual growth and democratic citizenship.

Simmons et al. (2015) describe how young people identified creative pedagogies as an important aspect of wellbeing in school. Thus we can see that there is a positive reciprocal feedback between emotional wellbeing and pedagogy. Rather than addressing emotional wellbeing as a separate set of skills that serves learning we can see that a positive learning experience can enhance emotional wellbeing and vice versa. In other words, one of the important things that a teacher can do to enhance emotional wellbeing is to be a caring and inclusive teacher. This can be seen as one of the conversion factors that will help young people to convert the capability of education into the functioning of learning.

The Capability Approach values human agency and self-determination, as it requires that people are able to recognise and pursue those things that they value, and it is therefore children should have opportunities to participate in decisions (Ballet et al. 2011). This as seen as important in a future-orientated sense as children learn the skills of decision making and the implications and consequences of choices, but it is also important in the present as children can make choices that bring meaning to their current lives. Again this has pedagogical implications. By inviting children's views on what and how they are to learn teachers can contribute to children feeling a sense of value and purpose in their educational endeavours. This was illustrated by Belinda, a primary school teacher participating in this study who saw her role in promoting children's wellbeing as very much located in the pedagogical choices that she made. Participatory pedagogies not only enhance children's emotional wellbeing (Simmons et al. 2015), they contribute to a eudaimonic sense of wellbeing, for children in the present, through learning which has meaning and purpose.

What is described in Belinda's account of her approach to teaching and learning was a dialogic approach in which she listened to the voices of children in order to direct her own choices about how to address a topic. This is a description of the dialogic relationship of care, predicated on shared trust and joint endeavour between teacher and learners characterised by Noddings (2005a, 2012) as 'true care', where the teacher is interested in the expressed need and interests of children, not the needs assumed by the school or the curriculum. This is a caring relationship that is strengthened by positive relations of working together. It is both the bedrock and the outcome of an inclusive pedagogical approach.

When considering the eudaimonic freedoms that can be achieved through education, pedagogical implications again come to the fore. Nussbaum (2006) argues that an education for Capability must focus on freedom of the mind. Rejecting forms of learning that focus solely on predetermined outcomes, or are over-reliant on memory she argues that:

> *Education must begin with the mind of the child and it must have a goal for increasing that mind's freedom in its social environment rather than killing it off' p 393*

Instead she encourages pedagogical approaches that encourage critical thinking, that promote democracy through and awareness of 'world citizenship' and narrative imagination, cultured through artistic and expressive education. In order to support children and young people to be able to make well-informed and rational choices about those things that are of value in life they need to be provided with opportunities to develop their critical powers of analysis and to understand the implications of their choices for others.

In viewing education as the means by which children develop the skills and knowledge that enhance their substantive freedoms to recognise and lead a life of value, questions must be raised about what is taught as well as how it is taught. What sort of knowledge and skills contribute to a life of value? Strong arguments are made for the contribution of creative arts to human flourishing. For example, Nussbaum (2006 p. 391) argues that they are 'crucial sources of both freedom and community', as we can learn to empathise with others and develop our critical thinking both through our own creative work and through studying the work of others. Similarly, Suissa (2008) argues that it is through the artistic expressions of others that we can come to better understand our own emotional responses to life. This was recognised by the English teacher, Graham, in this study who identified that through literature his pupils were able to consider 'big' issues such as love and death, and that through their literacy they were able to explore their own responses to life's events.

The eudaimonic role of creativity was highlighted an Australian study which argued that through creating and performing in their teacher education course, student teachers could 'move young people towards what is both life affirming and life enhancing' (Wright and Pascoe 2015 p. 304). Here, creativity was valued for its democratising role as described above, but also for the sense of personal fulfilment to be gained from intense imaginative working or exploring the work of others. In arguing that education is about 'learning to be human' Macmurray (2012) singled out the arts as a key to our capacity for sense experience, to recognise what is graceful and lovely in human life. Not only do the arts support us in our exploration and understanding of the messy word of human emotions, relationships and politics, they can be a source of great joy (Nussbaum 2006).

Similarly, the humanities are valued for the insight that they provide for our understanding of our interactions with others. Through history, politics, and social subjects, pupils can learn empathy and gain a critical perspective of the effects of their lives on others. A policy actor, Margaret pointed out in an interview 'How can you study World War II without considering man's inhumanity to man?' As Macmurray (2012) commented, our relations with others is a measure of our humanity and conversely 'inhumanity is the perversion of human relations' (p670). Interestingly, the literature on education for Capability is less forthcoming about the value of other subjects, for example sciences or mathematics for human flourishing. This seems to be partly driven by a justifiable sense that, in a profit driven age, arts and humanities are under threat of being side-lined, and their loss from the curriculum would indeed leave a very unbalanced educational experience (Nussbaum 2010).

Nonetheless is seems clear that any educational experience that enhances children's knowledge of the world and widens their range of possible beings and doings can bring value to their lives. Education is of intrinsic importance and being widely educated across a range of disciplines is a source of fulfilment in itself. This is captured by Griffiths (2012) who identifies the 'joy' of learning as an example of eudaimonia suggesting that fulfilment through learning can be one of life's true pleasures. This is illustrated by an example from a science curriculum that refers to the 'wonder' of looking at the night sky. This sense of delight through learning, is described as emerging from shared endeavour, between teacher and pupil as they work together towards a common goal of new understandings. Again we can see how the relationships between teachers and learners are supportive of the learning process, but equally they are intensified by the shared sense of achievement through working together. Learning takes place best in an environment of trust and care, but that environment is both a precursor and a product of learning.

This section has shown how, using the Capability approach as an evaluative space it is possible to integrate the multiple and complex relationships between education, wellbeing and social justice into a more comprehensive and cohesive understanding. By distinguishing between the freedom to participate fully in education and the freedoms that are achieved through education, we can see that physical, social and emotional wellbeing can be seen as functionings that allow access to the capabilities that can be achieved through education. Hence, it is imperative that teachers adopt caring pedagogical approaches that account for affective aspects of learning and value the dignity of individuals within the community of the classroom, in order that all children can engage with the learning. At the same time education is valued for its eudaimonic effects: it is through education that children develop the skills and knowledge to understanding of what for them is a valuable life, it is through education that they develop an understanding of their democratic obligations in both local and global communities, and it is through education that they learn to express themselves and understand the expressions of others. Furthermore, both the process of learning and becoming a better educated person have intrinsic value for human flourishing. The caring ethos of the classroom is the foundation of an inclusive pedagogy, but it is, in turn, greatly enriched by the positive experiences of learning together.

In previous chapters it was argued that, in the interagency landscape, discourses of wellbeing had migrated into education from other professional and academic groups policy to overshadow the discourse of education as a source of human flourishing. Teachers were being called upon to pay attention to the physical, social and emotional wellbeing of children, by creating a caring ethos, in policies that paid little heed to the actual process of learning and teaching. From this analysis, it is clear that the teaching profession has a unique contribution to make to wellbeing, in all its forms. Through sensitive pedagogies and interesting learning experiences teachers can vastly enhance the quality of human life through the experience of education. This is not to disregard the importance of affective wellbeing in education, but it is a mistake to focus on these discourses of wellbeing at the expense of eudaimonic considerations of education. Rather than expecting skills of social and emotional self-management to act as props to whatever learning is on offer, there are questions to be asked about how learning and teaching should be organised in the spirit of 'true care' to deliver the types of freedoms envisaged by the Capability Approach.

9.3 A Final Note

By taking a critical approach to discourse analysis, it has been revealed how language is used in the current hegemony of school-based wellbeing. By exploring the complexity of the 'milling mass' of discourses (Jager and Maier 2009) that coalesce around the term wellbeing this study shows how a single appealing word, in widespread policy use, can a convey multiple meanings. It shows how seemingly attractive terminology can be put to use by powerful groups to disguise agendas that may not serve the best interests of the children. It also shows how the discourses of wellbeing may change as they move between different groups and individuals; how some people may ascribe uncritically, and possibly unknowingly, to dominant ideologies and discourses whereas others may bring a more nuanced understanding to bear as they recontextualise policy discourses within their own system of knowledge and values. It highlights the dangers and the opportunities for equality in education.

Whilst this study has shown the slippery nature of language in relation to one attractive concept, it also has implications more generally for the critical examination of discourses in education policy. What are the other 'floating signifiers' in education that are universally seen as a good thing, and how are they adopted by different groups for different purposes? In more general terms this highlights the effect language can have, in influencing the behaviours of teachers and shaping the experiences of children, and urges caution in the way we use and understand the taken-for-granted phraseology in contemporary educational jargon.

Chapter 10
Appendix – Research Methods

The arguments developed throughout the book were informed by a research study which I conducted for my PhD. Rather than interrupt the flow of the discussions with details of the research methodology and methods, I have added extra detail here as an appendix, for those who may be interested in the structure of the study and the approaches taken to date collection and analysis.

The data collection was driven by three research questions. The first question was premised on the identification of discursive themes of wellbeing that were developed by an iterative process of to-ing and fro-ing between the literature and the emerging themes in the data, thereby using both inductive and deductive processes,

Research Question 1. *Using the five discursive themes of wellbeing in schools: How is health and wellbeing discursively represented in Scottish Educational policy, by members of the policy community and by teachers?*

This first question was demanding a descriptive discourse analysis of what could be identified in the data. The second question was more concerned with the purposes of the health and wellbeing policies in Scotland, in relation to learning, (in a wide sense of the word), and was concerned with the way in which health and wellbeing may be invoked in support of different policy aims. This then moved the analysis from the descriptive to the critical, as it began to reveal issues of power,

Research Question 2: *Which discourses are used to represent the relationship between learning and health and wellbeing, in written policy, and by policy actors and practitioners?*

The final research question was predicated on an expectation that the different discourses would not necessarily appear in the data as discrete entities, but that multiple discourses would interact in a complex and messy way,

Research question 3: *How do the different discourses interact?*

J. Spratt, *Wellbeing, Equity and Education*, Inclusive Learning and Educational Equity 1, DOI 10.1007/978-3-319-50066-9_10

A two stage study was conducted, firstly an analysis of the policy texts and secondly interviewing policy actors and teachers. I will now describe the approaches to data collection and then the approach analysis of data using Critical Discourse Analysis.

10.1 Data Collection

The data consisted of policy texts and interview data. I will describe the justification for the selection of policy texts, then outline the approaches taken to the interview phase of the study.

10.1.1 Identification of Policy Texts

The policy texts selected for inclusion in this study were all contemporary Scottish texts which related to children in the school context. Some of the texts were from stand-alone policy documents, whilst others were derived from the 'Curriculum for Excellence'. All Scottish Government texts which related to health and wellbeing in school were included in the analysis, as were the local authority policies from the two authorities forming the focus of this study. As this study focuses on the relationship between health and wellbeing and learning, some 'Curriculum for Excellence' material about learning was also relevant to the study. In particular, generic materials about curriculum design, or approaches to teaching and learning were selected, (rather than documents pertaining to specific curricular areas), to identify any references that might be made to wellbeing in these texts. Specifically, the texts were:

1. The Scottish Government's Economic Strategy (Scottish Government 2007b, 2011, 2015). The rationale for including the economic strategy in this study is twofold. Firstly, the interview undertaken with the representative of the Scottish Government's Learning Directorate (pseudonym Stephen) indicated that this was an important driver for the health and wellbeing policy. Secondly, there is a direct reference to the Economic Strategy in the *Getting it Right for Every Child* policy (Scottish Government 2008 p. 6). The current Scottish Nationalist government set out its economic framework in 2007, and updated this in 2011. Since many of the policies reviewed in this project emerged between 2007 and 2011, both of these documents are considered in the analysis.
2. Three key documents which guide the 'Getting it Right for Every Child' (GIRFEC) policy were considered. These are: *Getting it Right for Every Child: Guidance on the Child or Young Person's Plan*, (Scottish Executive 2007) and both editions of *A Guide to Getting it Right for Every Child* (Scottish Government 2008, 2012). This policy directs the interagency responses to situations when

children are thought to be experiencing difficulties in their lives. The GIRFEC approach is to 'promote action to improve the wellbeing of all children and young people' (Scottish Government 2008). In these documents eight 'areas of wellbeing' are identified, depicted as a 'wellbeing wheel'. The wellbeing wheel is also a central plank of the 'Curriculum for Excellence' policies, hence there is a direct intertextual link.

3. *The Curriculum for Excellence Building the Curriculum* series. This series of five papers was designed to support the roll out of the new curriculum. Two papers are of particular interest to this study as they have substantive sections about health and wellbeing. These are: *Building the Curriculum 1: The contribution of curriculum areas* (Scottish Executive 2006) and *Building the Curriculum 4: Skills for learning, skills for life and skills for work* (Scottish Government 2009).
4. Texts within the 'Curriculum for Excellence' which focus specifically on health and wellbeing. These are:
   - The health and wellbeing webpage on Education Scotland's 'Curriculum for Excellence' web-site
   - Curriculum for Excellence: Health and wellbeing across learning: responsibilities of all. Experiences and outcomes (Scottish Government n.d.-a)
   - Curriculum for Excellence: Health and wellbeing across learning: responsibilities of all. Principles and practice (Scottish Government n.d.-b)
5. The *Approaches to Learning* web pages in 'Curriculum for Excellence' which offer pedagogical guidance were studied to identify any ways that wellbeing is discursively invoked. These pages offer seven options: Active learning, ICT in learning, creativity, outdoor learning, co-operative and collaborative learning, peer education and Reggio Emilia.
6. The final documents considered in this section were the two health and wellbeing strategy documents produced by the participating local authorities. For reasons of anonymity these documents were referred to as: The Rural Council health and wellbeing strategy (2012) and The City Council health and wellbeing policy (2012). These are not formally cited in the book and do not appear in the reference list.

10.1.2 Sampling

Two phases of interviewing took place in this study, firstly involving representatives of the policy community and secondly involving teachers from four schools; two schools in each of two local authorities. Sampling was purposive; I was looking for people who were known to be active in this field and therefore able to discuss, in some depth, their ideas and understanding of the topic. The identification of individuals, school and local authorities to be invited to participate in the study depended, in part, upon the suggestions made by 'people in the know', and could be seen as a form of 'snowball sampling', or chain referral sampling. Snowball sampling is defined as a process whereby the researcher accesses participants through information provided by other participants (Noy 2008). The process begins with a small number of individuals from whom the ongoing referrals result in a chain, or series of chains. Usually snowball sampling is seen as a technique for accessing 'hard to reach' groups which may be networked informally, such as drug users or criminals (Atkinson and Flint 2001), and who maintain a low profile (Biernacki and Waldorf 1981). Whilst my sample was not drawn from the criminal underworld, it nonetheless relied on insider knowledge to locate institutions and individuals who are known to be proactive in a particular field. My participants were not deliberately hiding from view, yet at the same time they were difficult for an outsider to locate since there is no formal list or register from which information about practice could be drawn. For this reason, it was necessary to rely on the professional networks in which this knowledge resides. The snowball sampling therefore provided an approach that resonated theoretically with the purpose of the sampling.

10.1.3 The Sample

Representatives of the policy community were selected who held positions relating to children's health and wellbeing, which would have necessitated working closely with the 'Curriculum for Excellence'. At national level three participants were invited from education, two from health and one participant from the voluntary sector, representing a children's charity. Whilst some of the organisations and personnel to be included were predetermined, based on personal knowledge of the policy structures in health and education in Scotland, others were located through recommendation, by asking participants if to identify other key people at policy level.

Administratively Scotland is divided into 32 local authority areas. All state funded schools are under the direct control of their local authority, who will play a key role in interpreting policy, devising local guidelines and strategies that align with national policy. It was therefore important to include local policy actors in the study, as this was seen as, potentially, another stage at which policy could be reinterpreted on its journey from national government to the local school. This selection was informed by asking the national level policy actors which authorities they felt had been most active in the area of health and wellbeing. Two local authorities were invited to participate, which will be referred to as City Authority and Rural Authority. In each authority it had been intended to interview the Quality Improvement Officer (QIO) (or equivalent) with responsibility for health and wellbeing, and also to interview the counterpart in the local National Health Service (NHS) with responsibility for schools. However, only City Authority could identify an appropriate NHS contact. (In fact City Authority identified two people holding a job share, who elected to come together to the only paired interview of the study). Rural Authority partnered a health board which had closed the post of school liaison officer in a recent re-organisation, so no suitable representative of the health board existed in that area at that time. Details of the individuals involved are tabulated in Chap. 8.

Selection of schools was informed by the local authority representatives of each local authority who were in a position to advise on which schools were active in this work. One primary school and one secondary school was selected in each authority. Four members of the teaching staff were interviewed in each school. Again the selection of teachers to invite to participate relied on the insider knowledge of the head teacher, as to who was developing the field of 'health and wellbeing across learning', (as opposed to subject specialists who delivered the health and wellbeing curriculum). Details of the schools and teachers are outlined in Chap. 8.

10.1.4 Interviews

As this is a study of discourse, interested in how the participants verbally represented their understanding of the educational function of the health and wellbeing policy, interviewing was the most suitable method. The purpose of the research was to explore the language the study participants used when they talked about the policy, not what they actually did. Hence there was no attempt to study the practice of teachers through, for example, observation.

The interviews were mainly conducted as one-to-one face to face interviews, lasting between 30 and 55 min. Two interviews with policy actors were conducted over the telephone instead of face-to face, for reasons of pragmatism. With the interviewees' permission the interviews, including telephone interviews, were recorded. One participant, Fiona (Rural Academy, guidance teacher), did not wish to be recorded, so extensive notes were taken instead. Consequently, the study does not contain direct quotes from Fiona, but the notes were analysed in a similar way to the interview transcripts. The interviews were recorded on a high quality digital device, giving clear audio recordings, and were professionally transcribed.

Schostak (2006) comments that the initial moments in the interview encounter are important for setting a relaxed tone and developing an easy relationship. Upon meeting the interviewees, a number of preliminaries were followed, in an attempt to set the interviewee at ease, and to ensure that he/she understood and was happy with the purposes and procedures of the research. Although interviewees had received an information sheet and signed a consent form in advance, the initial moments were spent discussing the purpose of the individual interview within the context of the study as a whole and offering an opportunity to ask questions. Assurances of confidentiality, anonymity, right to withdraw at any point (including after the interview), were reiterated and permission to record was confirmed.

The start of the recorded interview was also designed as an 'ice breaker'. The first request was a very general enquiry about the interviewee, sometimes phrased informally as, 'tell me a bit about yourself'. This served several purposes, not least of which was to convey a message of interest in the interviewee as an individual (Luker 2008). This approach allowed participants to introduce themselves on their own terms and provided a few minutes to relax as they responded to a straightforward question. Usually they took the opportunity to say something about their recent professional experience, and their current responsibilities, which provided a helpful context for the later conversation. Policy actors, if necessary, were prompted to talk about their professional background prior to working in the policy arena.

Luker (2008) suggests that in undertaking interviews we should not ask directly what we want to know, but we should phrase our questions in ways that make sense to the interviewee. The main things that I wanted to know were ‘which discourses do you ascribe to?’ or ‘what is your ideological position?’ which clearly required some modification. The purpose of the interviews was really to provide a space and some stimulus for the interviewees to talk at some length around the subject, in order that I had some material on which to conduct a discourse analysis. The interviews were organised into several topic areas which the interviewees may feel able to discuss.

Policy actors were asked about their views on the rationale for the policy links between learning and health and wellbeing, their interpretation of some aspects of policy, their conceptualisation of wellbeing, and implications for local authorities, schools and other partners. The interview ended with a catch-all question in case anything that they deemed to be important had been overlooked. Although these are ostensibly separate areas of discussion, they all provided opportunities for the interviewees to reveal their discursive practices in this area. The range of topics and the length of the interview provided scope for different perspectives (if they existed) to be expressed.

In the case of teachers, the main bulk of the interview was based on a discussion of examples of the teachers’ practice. The topic of practice was a stimulus through which, it was hoped the teachers’ discourses would become apparent. The research interest was not in practice *per se*. Previous experience of working with teachers, both as a researcher and as a teacher educator led me to believe that teachers tend to be happy to talk extensively about their work, and this proved to be the case.

Towards the end of the interview all participants were asked ‘what do think wellbeing is?’ This was an important question for the study, but it is quite a difficult conceptual question, which could be off-putting to an interviewee who has not given much thought to the issue. Cohen et al. (2011) suggest that tricky questions should not be placed early in the interview, but should be saved until some rapport has been built up, and the interviewee has relaxed into the conversation. For that reason, this question was not asked until about three quarters of the interview had passed.

10.2 Using Critical Discourse Analysis

While CDA does not offer a rigid set of methods with which to interrogate texts, it does have some identifiable properties, which distinguish it from other approaches to discourse analysis. Most important is the requirement of criticality, involving normative judgements, whereby discourses are analysed in reference to a set of values (Fairclough 2010). In this case the discourses were analysed against two competing sets of values, the neoliberal and welfare-liberal conceptions of education, to see how the discourse of wellbeing was utilised in support of each. The purpose of the analysis was to unmask where the different ideologies were at play, and how they interacted in the education setting. Following Jager and Maier (2009) the study was using CDA to disentangle the 'milling mass' of discourses through a critical lens, considering the issues of power at play when policy seeks to shape some very personal aspects of children's lives.

CDA is transdisciplinary in nature (Fairclough 2003, 2010). The critique involved in CDA has been described as operating at different levels, drawing together different disciplines as it does so (Wodak 2009). The first stage of analysis, the 'text immanent critique' looks internally at the text for inconsistencies, paradoxes, contradictions within the discourse. The emphasis here is on the use of language to represent particular positions. This is a descriptive phase of the analysis simply looking to see what has been said and how it has been said. The text immanent critique took place at the level of the individual transcript, or policy document, to identify and map the ways in which wellbeing was represented and how it was discursively related to learning.

The second phase, the 'socio-diagnostic critique' seeks to demystify the text by drawing from a wider frame of social and political knowledge to demonstrate how the discourses are being used to serve ideological positions. This is the phase of interpretation of texts in terms of power. It is here that the researcher's own disciplinary background interacts with the linguistic analysis. In this study this is where knowledge of the wider literature was invoked to analyse the ideological purposes of the wellbeing policies, to identify the ways in which the different ideological positions interact, and to explore how discourses are recontextualised in different contexts.

For Wodak and Meyer (2009), a requirement of CDA is also a 'prognostic critique' which looks for ways in which this knowledge can be used to address inequalities which are exposed. A Critical Discourse Analysis does not stop with the identification of power imbalances, it tries to offer ways to improve the situation. In working with ideas drawn from from the Capability Approach to offer a more comprehensive understanding of wellbeing in schools, this book is attempting to offer an approach to the wellbeing of children that is embedded in notions of social justice. The prognostic critique can be found in the final chapter.

References

Acheson, D. (1998). *Independent inquiry into inequalities in health report*. London: The Stationery Office.

Adger, W. N., & Winkels, A. (2007). Vulnerability, poverty and sustaining well-being. In G. Atkinson, S. Dietz, & E. Neumayer (Eds.), *Handbook of sustainable development* (pp. 189–206). Cheltenham: Edward Elgar.

Agyeman, J. (2007). Environmental justice and sustainability. In G. Atkinson, S. Dietz, & E. Neumayer (Eds.), *Handbook of sustainable development* (pp. 171–188). Cheltenham: Edward Elgar.

Alkire, S. (2005). Why the capability approach? *Journal of Human Development and Capabilities, 6*(1), 116–133.

Alldred, P., & David, M. (2007). *Get real about sex*. Maidenhead: Open University Press.

Amerijckx, J., & Humblet, C. (2014). Child well-being: What does it mean? *Children and Society, 28*, 404–415.

Apple, M. (2006). *Educating the 'right' way. Markets, standards, God and inequality* (2nd ed.). Abingdon: Routledge.

Aristotle. (1985). *Nicomachean ethics*. Indianapolis: Hacket Publishing Company.

Arneil, B. (2002). Becoming vs being: A critical analysis of the child in liberal theory. In D. Archard & C. Macleod (Eds.), *The moral and political status of children* (pp. 70–94). Oxford: Oxford University Press.

Arthur, J. (2005). The re-emergence of character education in British education policy. *British Journal of Educational Studies, 53*(3), 239–254.

Ashton, J., & Seymour, J. (1988). *The new public health*. Buckingham: Open University Press.

Atkins, L., & Wallace, S. (2012). *Qualitative research in education*. London: Sage.

Atkinson, R., & Flint, J. (2001). *Accessing hidden and hard-to-reach populations: Snowball research strategies. social research update 33. Summer 2001*. Reading: Department of Sociology, University of Surrey.

Australian Institute of Health and Welfare. (2011). *Young Australians. Their health and wellbeing*. 2011-last update. Available: http://www.aihw.gov.au/WorkArea/DownloadAsset.aspx?id=10737419259 [Sept 16, 2016].

Ball, S. (2003). The teacher's soul and the terrors of performativity. *Journal of Education Policy, 18*(2), 215–228.

Ball, S. (2007). Big policies/small world. An introduction to international perspectives in education policy. In B. Lingard & J. Ozga (Eds.), *The RoutledgeFalmer reader in education policy and politics* (pp. 36–47). Abingdon: Routledge.

Ball, S. (2008). *The education debate*. Bristol: Policy Press.

J. Spratt, *Wellbeing, Equity and Education*, Inclusive Learning and Educational Equity 1, DOI 10.1007/978-3-319-50066-9

Ball, S., Maguire, M., & Braun, A. (2012). *How schools do policy: Policy enactments in secondary school*. London: Routledge.

Ballet, J., Biggeri, M., & Comim, F. (2011). Children's agency and the capability approach: A conceptual framework. In M. Biggeri, J. Ballet, & F. Comim (Eds.), *Children and the capability approach* (pp. 22–45). Palgrave Macmillan: Basingstoke.

Bates, R. (2007). Developing capabilities and the management of trust. In M. Walker & E. Unterhalter (Eds.), *Amartya Sen's capability approach and social justice in education* (pp. 138–155). Palgrave Macmillan: Basingstoke.

Bernstein, B. (1990). *The structuring of pedagogic discourse: Class codes and control* (Vol. IV). London: Routledge.

Bernstein, B. (2000). *Pedagogy, symbolic control and identity: Theory, research, critique* (2nd ed.). Oxford: Rowman and Littlefield Publishers Inc..

Biernacki, P., & Waldorf, D. (1981). Snowball sampling: Problems and techniques of chain referral sampling. *Sociological Methods and Research, 10*(2), 141–163.

Biesta, G. (2010). *Good education in an age of measurement: Ethics, politics, democracy*. Boulder: Paradigm Publishers.

Biggeri, M., & Santi, M. (2012). The missing dimensions of children's well-being and well-becoming in education systems: Capabilities and philosophy for children. *Journal of Human Development and Capabilities, 13*(3), 373–395.

Biggeri, M., Libanora, R., Mariani, S., & Menchini, L. (2006). Children conceptualising their capabilities: Results of a survey conducted during the First Children's World Congress on child labour. *Journal of Human Development and Capabilities, 7*(1), 59–83.

Blair, M., Stewart-Brown, S., Waterston, T., & Bryce, T. (2003). *Child public health*. Oxford: Oxford University Press.

Blake, S. (2008). There's a hole in the bucket: The politics, policy and practice of sex and relationships education. *Pastoral Care in Education, 26*(1), 33–41.

Brighouse, H. (2000). *School choice and social justice*. Oxford: Oxford University Press.

Brighouse, H. (2002). What rights (if any) do children have? In D. Archard & C. Macleod (Eds.), *The moral and political status of children* (pp. 31–52). Oxford: Oxford University Press.

Brighouse, H., & Unterhalter, E. (2010). Education for primary goods or for capabilities? In H. Brighouse & I. Robeyns (Eds.), *Measuring justice. primary goods and capabilities* (pp. 193–213). Cambridge: Cambridge University Press.

Burrows, L., & Wright, J. (2007). Prescribing practices: Shaping healthy children in schools. *International Journal of Children's Rights, 15*, 83–98.

Chitty, C. (2009). *Education policy in Britain* (2nd ed.). Basingstoke: Palgrave Macmillan.

Cigman, R. (2012). We need to talk about well-being. *Research Papers in Education, 27*(4), 449–462.

Clack, B. (2012). What difference does it make? Philosophical perspectives on the nature of well-being and the role of educational practice. *Research Papers in Education, 27*(4), 497–512.

Cockburn, T. (2011). Children, the feminist ethic of care and childhood studies: Is this the way to the good life? In S. Andresen, I. Diehm, U. Sander, & H. Ziegler (Eds.), *Children and the good life, children's well-being: Indicators and research* (Vol. 4, pp. 29–39). Heidelberg: Springer Science and Business Media.

Cohen, L., Manion, L., & Morrison, K. (2011). *Research methods in education* (7th ed.). London: Routledge.

Coleman, J. (2009). Well-being in schools: Empirical measure or politician's dream? *Oxford Review of Education, 35*(3), 281–292.

Coppock, V. (2005). Mad, bad or misunderstood. In H. Hendrick (Ed.), *Child welfare and social policy* (pp. 285–300). Bristol: Policy Press.

Coppock, V. (2010). Cause for hope or despair? Limits to theory and policy in relation to contemporary developments in promoting health and well-being in schools in the UK and implications for children's rights. *Advances in School Mental Health Promotion, 3*(1), 52–62.

Craig, C. (2007). *The potential dangers of a systematic, explicit approach to teaching social and emotional skills (Seal). An overview and summary of the arguments*. Glasgow: Centre for Confidence and Well-Being.

Cunningham, H. (2006). *The invention of childhood*. London: BBC Books.

Deci, L., & Ryan, R. (2008). Hedonia, eudaimonia and well-being: An introduction. *Journal of Happiness Studies, 9*, 1–11.

Department of Children, Schools and Families. (2003). *Every child matters*. 2003-last update. Available: https://www.gov.uk/government/uploads/system/uploads/attachment_data/file/272064/5860.pdf. [Sept 16, 2016].

Department of Education Northern Ireland. (2014). *Pupils emotional health and wellbeing*. 2014-last update. Available: https://www.education-ni.gov.uk/articles/imatter-programme. [Sept 16, 2016].

Diehm, I., & Magyar-Haas, V. (2011). Language education – For the "good life"? In S. Andresen, I. Diehm, U. Sander, & H. Ziegler (Eds.), *Children and the good life. Children's well-being: Indicators and research* (Vol. 4, pp. 103–113). Heidelberg: Springer Science and Business Media.

Dietz, S., & Rosa, E. (2009). Environmentally efficient wellbeing: Rethinking sustainability as the relationship between human wellbeing and environmental impacts. *Human Ecology Review, 16*(1), 114–123.

Dreze, J., & Sen, A. (1995). *India economic development and social opportunity*. New York: Oxford University Press.

Ecclestone, K. (2007). Resisting images of the 'diminished self': The implication of emotional well-being and emotional engagement in education policy. *Journal of Education Policy, 22*(4), 455–470.

Ecclestone, K. (2012). From emotional and psychological well-being to character education: Challenging policy discourses of behavioural science and 'vulnerability'. *Research Papers in Education, 27*(4), 463–480.

Ecclestone, K., & Hayes, D. (2009a). Changing the subject: The educational implications of developing emotional well-being. *Oxford Review of Education, 35*(3), 371–389.

Ecclestone, K., & Hayes, D. (2009b). *The dangerous rise of therapeutic education*. Abingdon: Routledge.

Education Scotland. (2016). *Curriculum for Excellence. a statement for practitioners from HM Chief Inspector of Education*. Livingston: Education Scotland.

Education Scotland. (n.d.). *Curriculum for Excellence* [Homepage of Scottish Government], [Online]. Available: http://www.educationscotland.gov.uk/learningandteaching/thecurriculum/. [Sept 16, 2016].

Ereaut, G., & Whiting, R. (2008). *What do we mean by "wellbeing"? And why might it matter? Research report DCSF – RW073*. London: Department of Children, Schools and Families and Linguistic Landscapes.

Evans, J., & Davies, B. (2012). Embodying policy Concepts. *Discourse; Studies in the Cultural Politics of Education, 35*(5), 617–633.

Evans, J., Davies, B., Rich, E., & Depian, L. (2013). Understanding policy: Why health education policy is important and why it does not appear to work. *British Educational Research Journal, 39*(2), 320–337.

Fairclough, N. (2003). *Analysing discourse. Textual analysis for social research*. Abingdon: Routledge.

Fairclough, N. (2010). *Critical discourse analysis: The critical study of language* (2nd ed.). Harlaw: Pearson Education Limited.

Federal Interagency Forum on Child and Family Statistics. (2016). *America's children in brief: Key national indicators of wellbeing, 2016*. [Homepage of Federal Interagency Forum on Child and Family Statistics], [Online]. 2016-last update. Available: http://www.childstats.gov/americaschildren/. [Sept 16, 2016].

Fielding, M. (2004). 'New wave' student voice and the renewal of civic society. *London Review of Education, 2*(3), 197–217.

Fielding, M. (2007). The human cost and intellectual poverty of high performance schooling: Radical philosophy, John Macmurray and the remaking of person-centred education. *Journal of Education Policy, 22*(4), 383–409.
Fielding, M. (2011). *Radical education and the common school: A democratic alternative*. London: Routledge.
Fielding, M. (2012). Education as if people matter: John Macmurray, community and the struggle for democracy. *Oxford Review of Education, 38*(6), 375–392.
Flores-Crespo, P. (2007). Situating education in the human capabilities approach. In M. Walker & E. Unterhalter (Eds.), *Amartya Sen's capability approach and social justice in education* (pp. 45–65). Palgrave Macmillan: Basingstoke.
Florian, L., & Black-Hawkins, K. (2011). Exploring inclusive pedagogy. *British Educational Research Journal, 37*(5), 813–828.
Foucault, M. (1973). *The birth of the clinic. An archaeology of medical perception*. London: Routledge.
Foucault, M. (1977). *Discipline and punish:The birth of the prison*. London: Penguin.
Foucault, M. (1979). *The history of sexuality. Volume 1: An introduction*. London: Allen Lane.
Foucault, M. (1984). The order of discourse. In M. Shapiro (Ed.), *Language and politics* (pp. 108–138). Oxford: Basil Blackwell.
Foucault, M. (1991). Governmentality. In G. Burchell, C. Gordon, & P. Miller (Eds.), *The Foucault effect: Studies in governmentality* (pp. 87–104). Hemel Hempstead: Harvester Wheatsheaf.
Fundacion Botin. (2015). *Social and emotional education. An international analysis. Fundacion Botin report 2015*. Santander: Fundacion Botin.
Furedi, F. (2004). *Therapy culture. Cultivating vulnerability in an uncertain age*. London: Routledge.
Furedi, F. (2005). *Politics of fear*. London: Continuum.
Gale, T., & Molla, T. (2015). Social justice intents in policy: An analysis of capability for and through education. *Journal of Education Policy, 30*(6), 810–830.
Gasper, D. (2004). *Human well-being. Concepts and conceptualisations, Working paper series No 388*. The Hague: Institute of Social Studies.
Gastaldo, D. (1997). Is health education good for you? Rethinking health education through the concept of bio-power. In A. Peterson & R. Bunton (Eds.), *Foucault, health and medicine* (pp. 113–133). London: Routledge.
Gillies, D. (2011). State education as high-yield investment: Human capital theory in European policy discourse. *Journal of Pedagogy, 2*(2), 224–245.
Giovanola, B. (2005). Personhood and human richness: Good and well-being in the capability approach and beyond. *Review of Social Economy, Lxiii*(2), 249–267.
Goleman, D. (1996). *Emotional intelligence*. London: Bloomsbury.
Gordon, J., & O'toole, L. (2015). Learning for well-being: Creativity and inner diversity. *Cambridge Journal of Education, 45*(3), 333–348.
Gould, S. (1996). *The mismeasure of man* (2nd ed.). London: W.W. Norton and Company Ltd.
Grek, S. (2009). Governing by numbers: The PISA 'effect' in Europe. *Journal of Education Policy, 24*(1), 23–37.
Griffiths, M. (2012). Why joy in education is an issue for socially just policies. *Journal of Education Policy, 27*(5), 655–670.
Grue, J. (2009). Critical discourse analysis, topoi and mystification. *Discourse Studies, 11*(3), 305–328.
Gustafsson, U. (2004). The privatisation of risk in school meals policies. *Health, Risk and Society, 6*(1), 53–65.
Hall, J., Sylva, K., Melhuish, E., Sammons, P., Siraj-Blatchford, I., & Taggart, B. (2009). The role of pre-school quality in promoting resilience in the cognitive development of young children. *Oxford Review of Education, 35*(3), 331–352.
Hallam, S. (2009). An evaluation of the Social and Emotional Aspects Of Learning (SEAL) programme: Promoting positive behaviour, effective learning and well-being in primary school children. *Oxford Review of Education, 35*(3), 313–330.

Hargreaves, A. (2016). *Leadership direction*. Keynote Paper. In: European conference for education research, Dublin. 24th August 2016.

Harris, B. (1995). *The health of the schoolchild. A history of the school medical service in England and Wales*. Buckingham: Open University Press.

Hart, S. (1998). A sorry tail: Ability, pedagogy and reform. *British Journal of Educational Studies, 46*(2), 153–168.

Hart, C. S. (2012). The capability approach and education. *Cambridge Journal of Education, 42*(3), 275–282.

Hart, S., Dixon, A., Drummond, M. J., & Mcintyre, D. (2004). *Learning without limits*. Maidenhead: Open University Press.

Helliwell, J., Layard, R., & Sachs, J. (2012). *World happiness report*. New York: The Earth Institute, Columbia University; Canadian Institute for Advanced Research, Centre for Economic Performance.

Henderson, K., & Tilbury, D. (2004). *Whole school approaches to sustainability: An international review of sustainable school programmes*. Canberra: Australian Research Institute on Education for Sustainability for the Department of the Environment and Heritage, Australian Government.

Hendrick, H. (1997). *Children, childhood and English society 1880–1990*. Cambridge: Cambridge University Press.

Hendrick, H. (2003). *Child welfare. Historical dimensions, contemporary debate*. Bristol: Policy Press.

Hendrick, H. (2005). Children and social policies. In H. Hendrick (Ed.), *Child welfare and social policy* (pp. 31–49). Bristol: Policy Press.

Hill, M., Davis, J., Prout, A., & Tisdall, K. (2004). Moving the participation agenda forward. *Children and Society, 18*(2), 77–86.

Huber, M., Knottnerus, A., Green, L., Van De Horst, H., Jadad, A., Kromhout, D., Leonard, B., Lorig, K., Loureiro, M., Van De Meer, J., Schnabel, P., Smith, R., Van Weel, C., & Smid, H. (2011). How should we define health? *British Medical Journal, 343*(D4163), 1–3.

Hudson, J., & Lowe, S. (2009). *Understanding the policy process*. Bristol: The Policy Press.

Humphrey, N. (2013). *Social and emotional learning: A critical appraisal*. London: Sage.

Jager, S., & Maier, F. (2009). Theoretical and methodological aspects of Foucauldian critical discourse analysis and dispotive analysis. In R. Wodak & M. Meyer (Eds.), *Methods of critical discourse analysis* (2nd ed., pp. 34–61). London: Sage.

John, P. (1998). *Analysing public policy*. London: Continuum.

Johnson, S., Gray, S., & Horrell, A. (2013). 'I want to look like that': Healthism, the ideal body and physical education in a Scottish secondary school. *Discourse; Studies in the Cultural Politics of Education, 34*(3), 457–473.

Kamens, D. (2013). Globalisation and the emergence of an audit culture: PISA and the search for 'best practices' and magic bullets. In H. Meyer & A. Benavot (Eds.), *PISA, power and policy: The emergence of global educational governance* (pp. 117–140). Oxford: Symposium Books.

Keyes, C. (2006). Subjective well-being in mental health and human development research world wide: An introduction. *Social Indicators Research, 77*, 1–10.

Kickbusch, I., Gordon, J., & O'Toole, L. (2012). *Learning for well-being: A policy priority for children and youth in Europe. A process for change. Drafted on behalf of the learning for well-being Consortium of Foundations in Europe*. Universal Education Foundation.

Knight, S. (2013). *International perspectives on forest schools. Natural places to play and learn*. London: Sage.

Layard, R. (2011). *Happiness. Lessons from a new science* (2nd ed.). London: Penguin.

Leggett, W. (2005). *After new labour: Social theory and centre left politics*. Basingstoke: Palgrave Macmillan.

Lindblom, C. (1959). The science of "muddling through". *Public Administration Review, 19*(2), 79–88.

Lingard, B. (2008). Scottish education: Reflections from an international perspective. In T. Bryce & W. Humes (Eds.), *Scottish education. Third edition: Beyond devolution* (pp. 968–981). Edinburgh: Edinburgh University Press.
Lingard, B., & Ozga, J. (2007). Reading education policy and politics. In B. Lingard & J. Ozga (Eds.), *The RoutledgeFalmer reader in education policy and politics* (pp. 1–8). Abingdon: Routledge.
Luker, K. (2008). *Salsa dancing into the social sciences. Research in an age of info-glut*. Cambridge, MA: Harvard University Press.
Lupton, D. (1995). *The imperative of health. Public health and the regulated body*. London: Sage.
Macleod, C. (2010). Primary Goods, Capabilities And Children. In H. Brighouse & I. Robeyns (Eds.), *Measuring justice. Primary goods and capabilities* (pp. 174–191). Cambridge: Cambridge University Press.
MacLure, M. (2003). *Discourse in educational and social research*. Buckingham: Open University Press.
Macmurray, J. (2012). Learning to be human. *Oxford Review of Education, 38*(6), 661–674.
Maddox, B. (2008). What good is literacy? Insights and implications of the capability approach. *Journal of Human Development, 9*(2), 185–206.
Maguire, C., Donovan, C., Mishook, J., De Gaillande, G., & Garcia, I. (2012). Choosing a life one has reason to value: The role of the arts in fostering capability development in four small urban schools. *Cambridge Journal of Education, 42*(3), 367–390.
Maguire, M., Braun, A., & Ball, S. (2015). 'Where you stand depends on where you sit': The social construction of policy enactments in the (English) secondary school. *Discourse; Studies in the Cultural Politics of Education, 36*(4), 485–499.
Maller, C., & Townsend, M. (2006). Children's mental health and wellbeing and hands-on contact with nature. *International Journal of Learning, 12*(4), 359–372.
Marmot, M. (2010). *Fair society, healthy lives*. London: The Marmot Review.
Matthews, G., Zeidner, M., & Roberts, R. (2004). *Emotional intelligence: Science and myth*. Cambridge, MA: MIT Press.
Mayall, B. (1996). *Children, health and the social order*. Buckingham: Open University Press.
Mayall, B. (1998). Towards a sociology of child health. *Sociology of Health and Illness, 20*(3), 269–288.
Mayall, B. (2000). The sociology of childhood in relation to children's rights. *The International Journal of Children's Rights, 8*(3), 243–295.
Mayall, B. (2001). Children's health at school. In P. Foley, J. Roche, & S. Tucker (Eds.), *Children in society: Contemporary theory, policy and practice* (pp. 195–201). Palgrave: Basingstoke.
Mayall, B. (2002). *Towards a sociology for childhood*. Buckingham: Open University Press.
Mclaughlin, C. (2015). *The connected school: A design for well-being* [Homepage of Pearson and NCB], [Online]. 2015-last update. Available: https://www.sussex.ac.uk/webteam/gateway/file.php?name=the-connected-school.pdf&site=26. [Sept 16, 2016].
Mill, J. S. (1861). Utilitarianism. In M. Warnock (Ed.), *Utilitarianism. John Stewart Mill*. Glasgow: Harpercollins.
Ministry of Education. (2007). *The New Zealand curriculum* [Homepage of Ministry of Education], [Online]. 2007-last update. Available: http://nzcurriculum.tki.org.nz/The-New-Zealand-Curriculum. [Sept 16, 2016].
Moore, S. (2012). Controlling passion? A review of recent developments in British sex education. *Health, Risk and Society, 14*(1), 25–40.
Morris, I. (2009). *Teaching happiness and well-being in schools: Learning to ride elephants*. London: Continuum.
Morrow, V. (2006). Understanding gender differences in context: Implications for young children's every day lives. *Children and Society, 20*(2), 92–104.
Morrow, V., & Mayall, B. (2009). What is wrong with children's well-being in the UK? Questions of meaning and measurement. *Journal of Social Welfare and Family Law, 3*(13), 217–229.
Nedovic, S., & Morrissey, A. (2013). Calm, active and focused: Children's responses to an organic outdoor learning environment. *Learning Environments Research, 16*, 281–295.

Noddings, N. (2005a). *The challenge to care in schools* (2nd ed.). New York: Teachers College Press.

Noddings, N. (2005b). What does it mean to educate the whole child? *Educational Leadership, 63*(1), 8–13.

Noddings, N. (2012). The caring relation in teaching. *Oxford Review of Education, 38*(6), 771–781.

Noy, C. (2008). Sampling knowledge: The hermeneutics of snowball sampling in qualitative research. *International Journal of Social Research Methodology, 11*(4), 327–344.

Nozick, R. (1974). *Anarchy, state and Utopia*. Oxford: Blackwell.

Nussbaum, M. (2003). Capabilities and fundamental entitlements: Sen and social justice. *Feminist Economics, 9*(2), 33–59.

Nussbaum, M. (2006). Education and democratic citizenship: Capabilities and quality education. *Journal of Human Development, 7*(3), 385–395.

Nussbaum, M. (2010). *Not for profit: Why education needs the humanities*. Princeton: Princeton University Press.

Nussbaum, M. (2011). *Creating capabilities. The human development approach*. Cambridge, MA: Belknap Press.

OECD. (2007). *Quality and equity of schooling in Scotland*. Paris: OECD.

Office for National Statistics. (2014). *Measuring national well-being – Exploring the well-being of children in the UK, 2014* [Homepage of Office for National Statistics], [Online]. 2014-last update. Available: http://www.ons.gov.uk/ons/rel/wellbeing/measuring-national-well-being/exploring-the-well-being-of-children-in-the-uk--2014/rpt-measuring-national-wellbeing-children-uk-2014.html. [Sept 16, 2016].

Office for National Statistics. (2016). *Measuring national wellbeing: Life in the UK: 2016* [Homepage Of Office For National Statistics], [Online]. 2016-last update. Available: http://www.ons.gov.uk/peoplepopulationandcommunity/wellbeing/articles/measuringnationalwellbeing/2016. [Sept 16, 2016].

Olssen, M., Codd, J., & O'Neill, A. (2004). *Education policy: Globalisation, citizenship and democracy*. London: Sage.

Ozga, J. (2000). *Policy research in educational settings*. Maidenhead: Open University Press.

Ozga, J., & Lingard, B. (2007). Globalisation, education, policy and politics. In B. Lingard & J. Ozga (Eds.), *The RoutledgeFalmer reader in education policy* (pp. 65–82). Abingdon: Routledge.

Paterson, L. (2003). *Scottish education in the 20th century*. Edinburgh: Edinburgh University Press.

Peterson, A., & Lupton, D. (1996). *The new public health. Health and self in the age of risk*. London: Sage.

Pickard, S. (2010). The 'Good Carer': Moral practices in late modernity. *Sociology, 44*(3), 471–487.

Plant, R. (2010). *The neo-liberal state*. Oxford: Oxford University Press.

Priestley, M. (2010). Curriculum for Excellence: transformational change or business as usual. *Scottish Educational Review, 42*(1), 23–36.

Priestley, M., & Humes, W. (2010). The development of Scotland's Curriculum for Excellence: Amnesia and deja vu. *Oxford Review of Education, 36*(3), 345–361.

Prout, A. (1999). Childhood bodies: Construction, agency and hybridity. In A. Prout (Ed.), *Body, childhood and society* (pp. 1–18). New York: Palgrave.

Prout, A., & James, A. (1997). A new paradigm for the sociology of childhood? Provenance, promise and problems. In A. James & A. Prout (Eds.), *Constructing and reconstructing childhood. Contemporary issues in the study of childhood* (2nd ed., pp. 7–33). London: Falmer Press.

Resnik, J. (2006). International organisations, the "Education-Economic Growth" black box and the development of world culture. *Comparative Education Review, 50*(2), 173–195.

Rezai-Rashti, G., Segeren, A., & Martino, W. (2016). *The new articulation of equity education in neoliberal times: The changing conception of social justice in Ontario*. Routledge/Taylor and Francis. doi:10.1080/14767724.2016.1169514.

Rizvi, F. (2004). Debating globalisation and education after September 11. *Comparative Education, 40*(2), 157–171.

Rizvi, F., & Lingard, B. (2010). *Globalising education policy*. London: Routledge.

Robeyns, I. (2003). Sen's capability approach and gender inequality: Selecting relevant capabilities. *Feminist Economics, 9*(2), 61–92.

Robeyns, I. (2005). The capability approach: A theoretical survey. *Journal of Human Development and Capabilities, 6*(1), 93–117.

Rogers, R. (2008). Critical discourse analysis in education. In M. Martin-Jones, A. De Mejia, & N. Hornberger (Eds.), *Encyclopaedia of language and education. Volume 3: Discourse and education* (2nd ed., pp. 53–68). Philadelphia: Springer Science and Business Media LCC.

Rose, N. (1999). *Governing the soul: The shaping of the private self* (2nd ed.). London: Free Association Books.

Rutkowski, D. (2007). Converging us softly: How intergovernmental organizations promote neoliberal educational policy. *Critical Studies in Education, 48*(2), 229–247.

Saito, M. (2003). Amartya Sen's capability approach to education: A critical exploration. *Journal of Philosophy of Education, 37*(1), 17–33.

Schostak, J. (2006). *Interviewing and representation in qualitative research*. Maidenhead: Open University Press.

Scott, G., & Mooney, G. (2009). Poverty and social justice in the devolved Scotland: Neoliberalism meets social democracy. *Social Policy and Society, 3*(4), 379–389.

Scottish Executive. (2004). *A Curriculum for Excellence; the Curriculum Review group*. Edinburgh: Scottish Executive.

Scottish Executive. (2006). *Building the curriculum 1: The contribution of curriculum areas* [Homepage of Scottish Executive], [Online]. 2006-last update. Available: http://www.educationscotland.gov.uk/Images/building_curriculum1_tcm4-383389.pdf. [Sept 16, 2016].

Scottish Executive. (2007). *Getting it Right for Every Child. Guidance on the child's or young person's plan*. Edinburgh: Scottish Executive.

Scottish Government. (2007a). *Schools (Health Promotion and Nutrition) (Scotland) Act*. Edinburgh: Scotland Government.

Scottish Government. (2007b). *The government economic strategy*. Edinburgh: Scottish Government.

Scottish Government. (2008). *A guide to Getting it Right for Every Child*. Edinburgh: Scottish Government.

Scottish Government. (2009). *Building the curriculum 4: skills for learning, skills for life and skills for work* [Homepage of Scottish Government], [Online]. 2009-last update. Available: http://www.educationscotland.gov.uk/Images/BtC4_Skills_tcm4-569141.pdf. [Sept 16, 2016].

Scottish Government, (2010). *Curriculum for Excellence through outdooor learning* [Homepage of Learning and Teaching Scotland], [Online]. 2010-last update. Available: http://www.educationscotland.gov.uk/Images/cfeoutdoorlearningfinal_tcm4–596061.pdf. [Sept 16, 2016].

Scottish Government. (2011). *The government economic strategy*. Edinburgh: Scottish Government.

Scottish Government. (2012). *A guide to Getting it Right for Every Child* [Homepage of Scottish Government], [Online]. 2012-last update. Available: http://www.scotland.gov.uk/Resource/0041/00419604.pdf. [Sept 16, 2016].

Scottish Government. (2013). *Better relationships, better learning, better behaviour* [Homepage of Scottish Government], [Online]. 2013-last update. Available: http://www.gov.scot/Publications/2013/03/7388/1. [Sept 16, 2016].

Scottish Government. (2015, March). *Scotland's economic strategy*. March 2015 [Homepage of Scottish Government], [Online]. 2015-last update. Available: http://www.gov.scot/Resource/0047/00472389.pdf [Sept 2016].

Scottish Government. (n.d.-a). *Curriculum for excellence: Health and wellbeing across learning. Responsibilities of all. Experiences and outcomes.* [Homepage of Scottish Government], [Online]. n.d.-a-last update. Available: http://www.educationscotland.gov.uk/Images/hwb_across_learning_experiences_outcomes_tcm4-540905.pdf. [Sept 16, 2016].

Scottish Government. (n.d.-b). *Curriculum for excellence: Health and wellbeing across learning. Responsibilities of all. Principles and practice* [Homepage of Scottish Government], [Online]. n.d.-b-last update. Available: http://www.educationscotland.gov.uk/Images/hwb_across_learning_principles_practice_tcm4-540402.pdf. [Sept 16, 2016].

Scottish Health Promoting Schools Unit. (2004). *Being well – Doing well. A framework for health promoting schools in Scotland.* [Homepage of Learning and Teaching Scotland], [Online]. 2004-last update. Available: http://www.educationscotland.gov.uk/Images/Beingwelldoingwell_tcm4-121991.pdf. [Sept 16, 2013].

Seligman, M. (2011). *Flourish. A new understanding of happiness and well-being and how to achieve them.* London: Nicholas Brealey Publishing.

Seligman, M., Ernst, R., Gillham, J., Reivich, K., & Linkins, M. (2009). Positive education; Positive psychology and classroom interventions. *Oxford Review of Education, 35*(3), 293–311.

Sellar, S., & Lingard, B. (2013). PISA and the expanding role of the OECD in global educational governance. In D. Meyer & A. Benavot (Eds.), *PISA, power and policy: The emergence of global educational governance* (pp. 185–206). Oxford: Symposium Books.

Sen, A. (1992). *Inequality reexamined.* Oxford: Oxford University Press.

Sen, A. (1999). *Development as freedom.* New York: Alfred A. Knopf, Inc.

Sen, A. (2006). *What clash of civilisations? Why religious identity isn't destiny.* 2006-Last Update. Available: http://www.slate.com/id/2138731 [Sept 16, 2016].

Sen, A. (2009). *The idea of justice.* London: Penguin.

Shucksmith, J., Spratt, J., Philip, K., & Macnaughton, R. (2009). *A critical review of the literature on children and young people's views of factors that influence their mental health.* Edinburgh: NHS Health Scotland.

Simmons, C., Graham, A., & Thomas, N. (2015). Imagining an ideal school for wellbeing: Locating student voice. *Journal of Educational Change, 16*, 129–144.

Singh, P., Thomas, S., & Harris, J. (2013). Recontextualising policy discourses: A Bernsteinian perspective on policy interpretation, translation, enactment. *Journal of Education Policy, 28*(4), 465–480.

Sosu, E., & Ellis, S. (2014). *Closing the attainment gap in Scottish education.* York: Joseph Rowntree Foundation.

Spratt, J. (2016). Childhood wellbeing: What role for education? *British Educational Research Journal, 42*(2), 223–239.

Spratt, J., & Florian, L. (2015). Inclusive pedagogy: From learning to action. Supporting each individual in the context of 'everybody'. *Teaching and Teacher Education, 49*, 89–96.

Spratt, J., Shucksmith, J., Philip, K., & Watson, C. (2006). 'Part of who we are as a school should include responsibility for well-being': Links between school environment, mental health and behaviour. *Pastoral Care in Education, 24*(3), 14–21.

Spratt, J., Shucksmith, J., Philip, K., & Mcnaughton, R. (2013). Active agents of health promotion? The school's role in supporting the HPV vaccination programme. *Sex Education, 13*(1), 82–95.

Stewart Burgher, M., Barnekow Rasmussen, V., & And Rivett, D. (1999). *The European network of health promoting schools – The alliance of education and health.* Denmark: Council of Europe, World Health Organisation Europe, European Commission.

Suissa, J. (2008). Lessons from a new science? On teaching happiness in schools. *Journal of Philosophy of Education, 42*(3–4), 575–590.

The Children's Society. (2015). *The good childhood report 2015* [Homepage of The Children's Society], [Online]. 2015-last update. Available: https://www.childrenssociety.org.uk/sites/default/files/TheGoodChildhoodReport2015.pdf. [Sept 16, 2016].

Townsend, P., & Davidson, N. (Eds.). (1982). *Inequalities in health. The black report.* London: Penguin.

UNICEF Innocenti Research Centre. (2007). *Child poverty in perspective: An overview of child wellbeing in rich countries. Innocenti report card 7*. Florence: UNICEF Innocenti Research Centre.
UNICEF Office of Research. (2013). *Innocenti report card 11. Child well-being in rich countries. a comparative overview*. Florence: UNICEF Office of Research.
United Nations. (1989). *Convention on the rights of the child*. Geneva: United Nations.
Unterhalter, E. (2003). The capabilities approach and gendered education: An examination of South African complexities. *Theory and Research in Education, 1*(1), 7–22.
Unterhalter, E., & Walker, M. (2007). Conclusion: Capabilities, social justice and education. In M. Walker & E. Unterhalter (Eds.), *Amartya Sen's capability approach and social justice*(pp. 239–253). Palgrave Macmillan: Basingstoke.
Uprichard, E. (2008). Children as 'Beings and Becomings': Children, childhood and temporality. *Children and Society, 22*, 303–313.
Van Dijk, T. A. (1993). Principles of discourse analysis. *Discourse and Society, 4*(2), 249–283.
Van Dijk, T. A. (1997). Discourse as interaction in society. In T. A. Van Dijk (Ed.), *Discourse as social interaction* (pp. 1–37). London: Sage.
Van Dijk, T. A. (2006a). Discourse, context and cognition. *Discourse Studies, 8*(1), 159–177.
Van Dijk, T. A. (2006b). Ideology and discourse analysis. *Journal of Political Ideologies, 11*(2), 115–140.
Van Leeuwen, T. (2009). Discourse as the recontextualisation of social practice. In R. Wodak & M. Meyer (Eds.), *Methods of critical discourse analysis* (2nd ed., pp. 144–161). London: Sage.
Vandenroeck, M., & Bouverne-De Bie, M. (2006). Children's agency and educational norms. A tensed negotiation. *Childhood, 13*(1), 127–143.
Waite, S. (2010). Losing our way: The downward path for outdoor learning for children aged 2–11 years. *Journal of Adventure Education and Outdoor Learning, 10*(2), 111–126.
Walker, M. (2005). Amartya Sen's capability approach and education. *Educational Action Research, 13*(1), 103–110.
Walker, M. (2006). Towards a capability-based theory of social justice for education policy making. *Journal of Education Policy, 21*(2), 163–185.
Walker, M., & Unterhalter, E. (2007). The capability approach: Its potential for use in education. In M. Walker & E. Unterhalter (Eds.), *Amartya Sen's capability approach and social justice in education* (pp. 1–17). Palgrave Macmillan: Basingstoke.
Watson, D., Emery, C., & Bayliss, P. (2012). *Children's social and emotional wellbeing in schools: A critical perspective*. Bristol: The Policy Press.
Weare, K. (2000). *Promoting mental, emotional and social health: A whole school approach*. Abingdon: Routledge.
Weare, K. (2004). *Developing the emotionally literate school*. London: Sage.
Weare, K. (2010). Mental health and social and emotional learning: Evidence, principles, tensions, balances. *Advances in School Mental Health Promotion, 3*(1), 5–17.
Weare, K., & Nind, M. (2011). Mental health promotion and problem prevention in schools: What does the evidence say? *Health Promotion International, 26*(S1), I29–I69.
Welsh Government. (2011). *Well-being*. 2011-last update. Available: http://wales.gov.uk/topics/educationandskills/schoolshome/wellbeing/?lang=en. [Sept 16, 2016].
White, J. (2011). *Exploring well-being in schools. A guide to making children's lives more fulfilling*. Abingdon: Routledge.
Wilkinson, R., & Pickett, K. (2010). *The spirit level. Why equality is better for everyone*. London: Penguin.
Winter, C. (2012). School curriculum, globalisation and the constitution of policy problems and solutions. *Journal of Education Policy, 27*(3), 295–314.
Wodak, R. (2008). Introduction. Discourse studies – Important concepts and terms. In R. Wodak & M. Krzyzankowski (Eds.), *Qualitative discourse analysis in the social sciences*. Palgrave Macmillan: Basingstoke.
Wodak, R. (2009). The semiotics of racism. In J. Renkema (Ed.), *Discourse, of course*(pp. 311–326). Amsterdam: John Benjamin Publishing Company.

Wodak, R., & Meyer, M. (2009). Critical discourse analysis: History, agenda, theory and methodology. In R. Wodak & M. Meyer (Eds.), *Methods of critical discourse analysis* (2nd ed., pp. 1–33). London: Sage.

Wood, D., & Deprez, L. S. (2012). Teaching for human well-being: The curricular implications for the capability approach. *Journal of Human Development and Capabilities, 13*(3), 471–493.

World Health Organisation. (1948). *Constitution*. Geneva: World Health Organisation.

World Health Organisation. (1986). *Ottowa charter for health promotion.* In: First international conference on health promotion. Ottowa, 21 November 1986. WHO/HPR/HEP/95.1. Copenhagen: World Health Organisation.

World Health Organisation. (1998). *Health promoting schools: A healthy setting for living, learning and working*. Geneva: World Health Organisation.

Wright, P., & Pascoe, R. (2015). Eudaimonia and creativity: The art of human flourishing. *Cambridge Journal of Education, 45*(3), 295–306.

Wyness, M. (2001). Children, childhood and political participation: Case studies of young people's councils. *The International Journal of Children's Rights, 9*(3), 193–212.

MIX
Papier aus verantwortungsvollen Quellen
Paper from responsible sources
FSC® C105338

If you have any concerns about our products,
you can contact us on
ProductSafety@springernature.com

In case Publisher is established outside the EU,
the EU authorized representative is:
Springer Nature Customer Service Center GmbH
Europaplatz 3, 69115 Heidelberg, Germany

Printed by Libri Plureos GmbH
in Hamburg, Germany